DEADLY DECEPTION

"Pull over there Jon," Jeremiah Rodgers shouted.

Jon Lawrence pulled over obediently and stopped. Rodgers turned to Jennifer Robinson excitedly.

"You have to see this," he said. "There are pot plants!"

"Pot plants?" Jennifer asked.

"Yes!" and Rodgers got out and walked down the hill.

"Right down there," said Rodgers pointing off into the darkness.

Rodgers waited until she had just passed him, then reached into his waistband and pulled out the pistol. He raised the gun, leveled it at the back of her head.

The pistol discharged with a sharp crack into the night.

FLESH COLLECTORS

FRED ROSEN

PINNACLE BOOKS
Kensington Publishing Corp.
http://www.kensingtonbooks.com

Some names have been changed to protect the privacy of individuals connected to this story.

PINNACLE BOOKS are published by

Kensington Publishing Corp.
850 Third Avenue
New York, NY 10022

All Kensington Titles, Imprints and Distributed Lines are available at special quantity discounts for bulk purchases for sales promotions, premiums, fund-raising, and educational or institutional use. Special book excerpts or customized printings can also be created to fit specific needs. For details, write or phone the office of the Kensington special sales manager: Kensington Publishing Corp., 850 Third Avenue, New York, NY 10022, attn: Special Sales Department, Phone: 1-800-221-2647.

Pinnacle and the P logo Reg. U.S. Pat. & TM Off.

First printing: December 2003
10 9 8 7 6 5 4 3 2

Printed in the United States of America

For Don

It is not funny that a man should be killed, but it is sometimes funny that he should be killed for so little, and that his death should be the coin of what we call civilization.

—Raymond Chandler,
"The Simple Art of Murder"

PROLOGUE

1998

It was spring and large oak, pine and magnolia trees were beginning to bloom on the streets of Milton, Florida. Almost every yard was ablaze with the colorful blooms of the azalea and the camellia. It was always that way, even in the early 1800s when legendary highwayman Joseph Hare held sway in the area.

Census estimates put Milton's present-day population at over seven thousand residents for the roughly five-square-mile city. The county seat for Santa Rosa County, Milton's downtown is a collection of dilapidated early-twentieth-century buildings that are struggling to decide whether to collapse against the weight of a century of river air and hurricanes.

On one side of the town is the Blackwater River. A few miles south is the Gulf of Mexico. In between are neat one-family ranch homes, trailers, and up on the main drag of Route 90, Hungry Howie's Pizza & Subs, Leather Works Plus, Papa John's Pizza and Bill's Tattoos and Piercings. There's more of the usual suburban collection of fast-food joints and shopping malls. Wal-Mart is a major hangout.

Tropical storms and hurricanes regularly roll in from the Gulf during the early fall. The torrential rains combined with the soft ground make the whole area a swamp, but the late fall and winter months more than compensate with warm temperatures and tropical breezes. A whole culture has grown up around the area that the locals call "the Redneck Riviera" or "Lower Alabama." Despite hurrican season that lasts from August through September, the Gulf's warm water and beaches bring the area millions in tourist business from Alabama, which is directly north.

Down Norris Road is Pace, the town's high school. Its corridors are festooned with multicolored crepe paper in the school's patriotic colors of red, white and blue, celebrating the team's athletic accomplishments. While the schools in the county boast a decent 16.7 to 1 student/teacher ratio, Pace's average SAT scores, at 1056, are only slightly above the national average. The kids from Pace do not have an easy road ahead of them.

A few miles away, on Spencer Field Road, is Spencer Outlying Field. A federal installation where navy copters do touch-and-go landings, Spencer's copters are served by the deployment of two-thousand-gallon JP5 fuel-servicing trucks. The airfield is a vast piece of scrub brush in the middle of Santa Rosa County, smack-dab in the middle of Milton. If a local were looking to dump a body, he would think this is a good spot. Considering the field's vastness, he could suppose the corpse might not be discovered for days.

Pace, Florida, a few miles down the road from Milton, is another small town in the Florida Panhandle. The Panhandle is an area of scrub brush and canebrake that extends east from the Alabama border, under Georgia, to the Atlantic Ocean. Pace was no different from any of those other towns—the kids were just as desperate to escape as their parents had been.

Some—the few who really excelled in the high school—might be able to use a college education to escape from their modern-day whitewashed ghetto. Others used business ability to become successful enough to get out of town. Still, others used their charm and good looks to net husbands and wives of greater fortune.

In Pace, everybody knows everybody. This is the South, with families going back generations, since before the Civil War. These people have great-grandfathers who fought for the Confederacy. The present-day inhabitants are still bearing the brunt of the poverty and hopelessness that followed their ancestors' defeat at Union hands. Buried deep within this proud community are a few families of which the others are wary—not very many, but a few never-the-less.

When a Pace resident says so-and-so came from a "bad line," he knows the entire family history stretching back generations. Such was the case with the surname Lawrence. It was spoken in hushed tones. By the time the spring of 1998 was over, the

Lawrence name would once again be spoken with dread, and for good reason.

Two people would be dead and horribly mutilated. One would be a victim of savagery and betrayal of the most heinous sort, the other necrophilia and attempted cannibalism. The killers would join Leopold and Loeb, who strangled poor Bobby Franks in 1924, and Hickock and Smith, who, in 1959, massacred the Clutter family of Kansas "in cold blood," to make the list of American history's infamous duos. Nearly forty years after Hickock and Smith's exploits, they made the savagery of their predecessors seem mild in comparison.

Their names were Rodgers and Lawrence. To some, they were known as the "flesh collectors."

PART ONE

Part One

CHAPTER 1

April 9, 1998

It was the kind of balmy night that made it hard to sleep. There was excitement in the air that crackled like the campfires spread throughout the Florida Panhandle. In cities, kids hang out on street corners; in the Panhandle, at campfires.

At first glance, Jeremiah Rodgers and Jonathan Lawrence didn't seem any different from the other twentysomething slackers in the Panhandle who stood around a campfire that night. Like most of their friends, they had gotten through high school with no particular destination in mind. Not having any special trade or skill, they were someplace in the middle, not knowing their way in life. Only these guys were different.

Both men had a variety of mental problems that had led to their being institutionalized in their early twenties. That, alone, distinguished the two of them from the general populace. But what made them even more unique was that they had been institutionalized at Chattahoochee, the once-infamous state mental hospital that specialized in treating the criminally insane.

Jeremiah Rodgers, nearly twenty-one years old, was a muscular, 5'7" slick-talking tattoo artist with a pencil-thin mustache that made him look like an oily version of Errol Flynn. He also resembled a sawed-off version of Eric Roberts, who played the sleazy husband in *Star 80.* His close older friend, almost twenty-three-year-old Jonathan Lawrence, was a pensive, moody man with a bland, round face that concealed the depravity he carefully kept hidden. Physically unattractive, he was a stocky five feet seven inches and 166 pounds. Over the years, he had learned how to handle a knife with amazing dexterity.

Looking for the answer to life's questions, they stood gazing into the fire that they had kindled awhile before. They listened to the wind in the canebrake as it made a mournful, rustling sound. They smoked a joint and thought back to just a few short hours ago.

That afternoon, Lawrence had called twenty-year-old Justin Livingston, his cousin. Justin visited frequently. Rodgers *hated* Justin. The big kid looked normal but wasn't. Rodgers didn't care that Justin took a variety of antipsychotic medication without which he could not function. He didn't care that Justin was one of life's lost souls and always would be. Not only did Rodgers not care, he wanted *to take the guy out*! Justin had been a thorn in Rodgers's side for too long.

Justin would come over to Lawrence's house asking for smokes, Pepsi, beer, whatever he could hustle. And Lawrence would always give his cousin something. Then Justin would sit down and enjoy his treat. The big kid had no common sense, and Rodgers just wanted him to get lost. Permanently. Lawrence, the quieter of the two, agreed with his partner.

Jon Lawrence's birthday was coming up in a few days. He and Rodgers reasoned it was as good an excuse as any to get Justin to come over. Not that they really needed to give him a special invite, but if they wanted to kill him, and if they were ready to do it, there was no time like the present. It was something they had been thinking about.

Jon Lawrence picked up the phone and dialed.

"Hello," answered a pleasant voice.

"Hey, Justin, it's Jon," said Lawrence.

"Oh, hey, Jon."

Justin was on federal disability and got a check every month from the government because his neurological problems prevented him from working. His mother, Elizabeth Livingston, was always trying to find a way to fill up his time. Frequently he accompanied her to work, but not that day, he told Lawrence. He had gotten just too damn bored following his mother around.

Jon Lawrence knew that it was good that Justin's mother wasn't around. It would give them time to get things done.

"Hey, Justin, why don't you come over? Jeremiah's giving me a party for my birthday."

Justin's emotional age had tested out to twelve

years old, and like most twelve-year-olds, Justin loved
parties. And he knew that his cousin's birthday was
coming up. Justin got all duded up for the party in
the cowboy clothes he favored. He put on a green
pinstriped cowboy shirt and snakeskin cowboy boots.
He loved Panhandle Slim boots too. His mother got
him a pair as a graduation present and he had only
worn them once, favoring his snakeskins instead.

Justin set off by foot. It was only a few blocks to
his cousin and his friend. But Justin never went anyplace directly. Justin liked to walk and made a
circuit of the community. He was a friendly guy who
liked saying hello to people. Justin waved at everyone he saw and made his little rounds, stopping,
chatting, waving and glad-handing like some politi-
cian on the stump.

All the neighbors along the way were friendly
too. They knew of Justin's disability and emotional
immaturity. Even when his mama had to work late
at the school, where she was a custodian, and Justin
was alone, there was always someone in the neighborhood who would look out for him and make
sure everything was okay.

Justin finally got to his cousin's that day and was
surprised; there was no party. But with reassurances
from both Lawrence and Rodgers that that would
come later, he settled down to hang out. It was a
warm day, so they lounged around in the backyard
with beers. The three young men watched as Ricky,
Lawrence's brother, and his uncle Roy worked on
Ricky's truck. At that exact moment, the very idea
to kill Justin Livingston had become a reality. In po-

lice parlance, it would be the moment the conspiracy to commit murder began.

When Justin looked away, Lawrence took his hand and drew it slowly across and around his throat. Rodgers later said he took the gesture to mean that "they were gonna take Justin out and do something to him." Saying nothing, Rodgers shrugged his thickly muscled, heavily tattooed shoulders. As the afternoon wore on and the shadows lengthened, the three left Ricky and Roy Lee to their outdoor labors, preferring to watch a movie on the VCR. Rodgers asked Justin if he wanted to smoke a joint and Justin, who liked weed, said, "Fire it up."

"Okay," Rodgers answered, "but we gotta wait until later on."

Rodgers went to the bathroom. When he came back, Lawrence told him, "We'll do it at the helicopter field." A few hours later, when Rick and Roy Lee had left and darkness had fallen across the Florida Panhandle, Rodgers pressed the stop button on the VCR; it was time to go.

The three got in the truck and rode straight to the helicopter field, parking by the side of the road. They got out and walked over the rough Florida grass. Unlike the grass used on lawns in northern climes, Florida residents use grass that can stand up to the harsh heat. It felt like a firm sponge as the men trampled it on the way to the fence. Lawrence took out a fence cutter and made a hole in the bottom of the fence. Staying low, they all crawled through.

"Where's the joint?" Justin asked.

"Got it right here," Rodgers answered, patting his coat pocket.

They ran out toward the tower in the middle of the field, deserted at this late hour.

"Where's the joint?" Justin repeated.

"What did you do wrong?'" Rodgers asked him grimly.

Justin noted the change in tone. He was going to get beaten up.

"I come out here?" Justin answered, perplexed. "Y'all ain't gonna hurt me, are you?" Justin asked.

"No," said Lawrence firmly to his cousin. "We're just sitting out here 'cause I'm not sure what Jeremiah wants to do."

"Can you see the stars, Justin?" Rodgers asked. "There's three stars that create a triangle. And in the middle of that triangle, if you can tell me the lesser or the lighter stars that form a picture, I'll give you twenty bucks."

"The reason I said that was to get him to look up so it would be easier to stab him," Rodgers later explained. "[But] I couldn't do it at that time, so eventually he gave up [looking]. The chance was gone."

They started walking back toward the truck.

"We'll smoke the joint on the way back," Rodgers reassured Justin.

For his part, Lawrence couldn't figure what was happening, except maybe Rodgers was playing one of his weird mind games. Suddenly Rodgers pivoted. He pulled up his black T-shirt and pulled the bowie knife from the waistband of his jeans. He turned on his Caterpillar steel-toed boots. The bowie knife flashed once in the moonlight and came down into Justin's back.

"Why'd you do that?" Justin asked. He was not angry, just confused—why would his friend stab him?

The knife had stopped someplace on the inside. To Rodgers, it felt like he had hit a bone and the knife glanced off it. The blow had knocked Justin all the way to the ground.

"Stay down on the ground and face down," Rodgers ordered. He threw the bowie knife away and turned to Lawrence. "Give me your knife."

Shocked at what had just happened, Lawrence waited a minute before handing over his knife.

"What are you gonna do? Are you gonna hurt me?"

"No," Rodgers answered, his voice honey sweet. "I'm not gonna hurt you. Lie down, just face down for a minute." Justin turned facedown to the ground. Rodgers didn't want to look at his face.

"Is this real?" Justin asked.

"No, it's not real," Rodgers answered, working up his nerve. "You're just on a bad [LSD] 'trip.'"

"All right."

Rodgers later related, "I crouched down beside him, and when I got my nerve up, I stabbed him between the shoulder blades with all the [knife] blade going through. I left the knife there for a second."

Justin struggled to get up. He got to his hands and his knees. He was in intense pain, the knife sticking out of his shoulder, the blood streaming down. Rodgers backed up a little bit with his hand still on the knife.

"Just lay down," Rodgers ordered.

Some part of Justin knew that was not a good idea and he struggled to stand, but Rodgers kept his hand on the knife, controlling him, maybe twisting it a little, until Justin finally sagged back down to the ground. Rodgers bent down and slowly pulled the knife out. It must have been intensely painful. He walked away, throwing the knife down as he went.

Lawrence grabbed the knife. He picked it up and tried to stab Justin, but he couldn't do it. He just stood there for a few moments, something holding him back.

"It's hard," Lawrence said. "I can't do it right now."

"Yeah, I know, it's hard, ain't it?" Rodgers answered.

During all that time, Justin was fully conscious, listening to every word.

"I gotta shit," Justin said suddenly.

Rodgers walked up to him.

"Can you breathe, Justin?"

Justin nodded his head.

"Can you see me?"

Justin turned and looked up with open eyes, then nodded weakly.

"Can you hear me?"

Another nod.

"Does it hurt?"

"Yeah."

"Worm," Rodgers called him.

"Worm" was the nickname Rodgers had given him. Justin hated it but couldn't stand up to him. Rodgers intimidated him. Between his tattoos, muscular build and sly smile, he didn't look like the kind of guy you wanted to cross. For Rodgers, it was a way to dehumanize Justin.

Justin had been kind and polite to him. Through his humanity, he had invaded the perimeter of Rodgers's psyche. Justin had made the mistake of getting too close to Rodgers without even realizing it. Rodgers wished that he would hurry up and die. He knelt down beside Justin to stab him again but couldn't get up the nerve. Lawrence just sat there. He couldn't really think of what to do, but he knew his cousin had been stabbed. Lawrence also knew that Justin was still alive.

He could hear him breathing, not talking, just breathing, a heap on the ground. He was breathing kind of slow. Rodgers never said anything. He and Lawrence just sat and looked pensively at the man who was dying. They listened to the bugs and then to Justin Livingston's dying breath. To Lawrence, it was kind of like a bad dream. He could never really tell when Justin died. He just kind of disappeared a little bit at a time.

Rodgers decided to hasten the process along.

"You got a towel or something?" Rodgers asked.

A few years before, Lawrence's mom had bought two red flannel shirts at a flea market, one of Florida's favorite cultural venues. He was wearing one, Rodgers the other. Without waiting for an answer to his question, Rodgers took his off and wrapped it around Justin's neck. Using it as a garrote, he pulled it tight and strangled Justin to make sure he was dead.

Jeremiah is strangling him to put him out of his misery, Lawrence thought. By his own estimate, Rodgers kept strangling Justin for three minutes, more than enough time to kill anyone, let alone someone who had already been fatally stabbed.

When it was over, Lawrence reached down to touch his cousin's neck. He felt really cold, so he just backed away from him and sat down for a little while. Lawrence then came back over and knelt down beside the lifeless body. He took the knife and stabbed Justin ten more times in the back, really quickly, enjoying mutilating his cousin.

"He did it real quick and then he quit. Wiped his knife on the grass, put it back in the sheath, got everything together and we ran back to Jon's truck," Rodgers would recount later.

Lawrence watched as Rodgers took out the bolt cutters and cut the fence down near the bottom and then moved the cutter upward, snipping metal as he went. Finished, he pulled the fence up and hooked it at the top so it would stay up. He had a hole big enough to drive a truck through. He ran a little way back into the field and he got the truck facing the hole. He clicked his lights on to see for a minute, and when he got through the fence, he turned them off. They drove out to where Justin was lying lifeless on the ground near the still-deserted control tower.

Lawrence pulled a blanket out of his truck and laid it on the ground. They rolled Justin inside it and then rolled him over so the blanket wrapped around him. Together, they picked him up and put him in the back of Lawrence's truck. They shut the tailgate, then went back to look on the ground for any evidence they might have left behind.

They picked up a few things, including Justin's cigarette lighter, a Coke can, the knives and Lawrence's eyeglasses that he had dropped while stabbing Justin. They left, driving through the same hole that they had cut. Then they went straight out into the more rural Chumuckla section of the county.

On the way, they stopped at a Tom Thumb convenience store. Lawrence had always wanted to try the Doritos 3D's chips, so he bought a bag, then drove out past the cotton gin to Sandy Landing. They sat out there for a little while, near the power lines, munching on the chips. After a few minutes, Lawrence put the truck in motion and they rode around a little bit.

They stopped in the middle of nowhere, near a little lake. They got out and stood leaning up against the pickup, just talking and looking up at the stars. It seemed to Lawrence that they stayed there like that for a good long while.

Like so many times in the past, they kindled a fire and looked into it, as if expecting a portent. Sometimes their gaze turned toward the heavens and then they came back to reality, listening to the wind in the canebrake, which made such a sad, stirring sound. When the wind died down, they could hear the bugs.

While Lawrence sat listening to the crickets, Rodgers got a shovel out of the truck. Lawrence kept it there because his father always told him to keep things in the truck that would help him in case of emergency, and he always tried to listen.

Rodgers dug, working up a sweat in the cool night air. He took off his shirt and continued digging. Rodgers never did get tired of digging the grave. Despite his height, which gave him a feeling of inferiority, he worked out and was immensely strong.

Finally they pulled out the blanket-clad body. Rodgers grabbed it by the collar, Lawrence by the boots. Rodgers pulled and Lawrence pushed and, pretty soon, Justin Lawrence's body was dragged into a cold hole in the ground. The legs were hard; the hole wasn't long enough, so they pushed his knees under his chin.

"The blanket came open and his face was like right there as I was putting him in the hole. And that's what keeps sticking in my head. His face was just real wet. It wasn't tears; it was like sweat just beaded all over his face, but it wasn't sweat," Rodgers said later.

It was the early hours of the morning and the heat of the oncoming day, when combined with cool surfaces, had caused dew to form. Because his body was cooling as it decomposed, dew had formed on Justin's skin. Even as they started covering him up with dirt, all Rodgers could see in his mind's eye was the dead man's face.

Sweating afterward, Lawrence leaned up against the truck and was trying to think, trying to realize what was happening. They drove away to a dark spot, made a fire and looked into it for a while until they got really thirsty. They got in the pickup and drove back out, back down to Tom Thumb. Lawrence had a little bit of change left and bought some Cokes and relaxed. As for Rodgers, he remembered that Justin's eyes had been open before they were covered by mounds of dirt. The image just wouldn't go out of his mind. In some small way, his conscience was eating at him.

They got back to Lawrence's house just as the sun was coming up. Rodgers remembered that he had left his beeper, wallet and all his change on Lawrence's couch. He had left it there so he wouldn't drop anything at what he knew was going to be the crime scene. He picked his stuff up and put it back in his pockets.

Lawrence kept his wallet on a chain attached to his belt. He patted his pocket to make sure it was still there; it was.

"I'm gonna wash the knives up," said Lawrence. He took the murder weapons as well as the flannel shirt Rodgers had used to strangle Justin and all the other evidence. Rodgers just assumed he was going to dispose of it. The two men didn't talk much.

"We didn't plan on any questions," Rodgers revealed. "We didn't plan on Justin being found."

* * *

It was funny about those eyeglasses, the ones Lawrence had almost left at the scene.

Seventy-four years before, at another crime scene in another state, investigators looked at the crumpled-up body of a young teenage boy who had been bludgeoned. The only clue left at the scene by the killers was a pair of eyeglasses. The glasses were later traced back to a nineteen-year-old genius named Nathan Leopold, whose best friend was Richard Loeb.

Having killed their fourteen-year-old neighbor, Bobby Franks, Leopold and Loeb became the country's most reviled murderers. Their attorney, the great Clarence Darrow, pleaded them guilty. Arguing for mercy before the judge during the penalty phase, Darrow succeeded. Leopold and Loeb beat death and were instead sentenced to life in prison. And the trial was all because of the glasses.

But the Santa Rosa police wouldn't have the benefit of Lawrence's eyeglasses at the crime scene, if they ever found it, as remote as it was. Lawrence had actually been smarter than the genius Loeb and removed all clues from the scene. Like Leopold and Loeb, who between them had committed only petty crimes until they killed Franks, Rodgers and Lawrence had just done together what they could never do alone.

The blending of their personalities was subtle. When they were together, no one noticed the change. Separately, they were nothing more than disturbed young men. Together, they were capable of anything, including murder.

CHAPTER 2

BAM! BAM!

Elizabeth Livingston and her boyfriend, Cory Liddell, heard two gunshots.

"Oh, Cory, I'm afraid that's Justin. Someone shot him!" she screamed. They ran outside to see what was going on. Walking up the street, they saw tire marks in the gutter.

"Cory, someone shot Justin and stuffed him in their trunk and rode away," said a fearful Livingston.

Returning to the small ranch house in the middle of Pace that she shared with her son, Elizabeth felt that fear in her heart that every parent dreads: her child might be dead. In most cases, it is an irrational fear that comes about because of some mistake, like a child running out of a movie theater without the parent or the child playing too close to traffic. But in Justin's case, it was real.

"Justin always comes home by seven o'clock to take his medication, but that day he didn't. I was worried. It wasn't like him to just disappear," she would later tell a reporter.

No, it wasn't. Justin knew he had problems that were controlled with medication. He didn't want to have the hallucinations again or be confined to a mental hospital against his will, as he had been. Elizabeth Livingston remembered Justin "coming down with schizophrenia" in high school.

"Felicia, his sister, has schizophrenia. She's twenty-six now," Elizabeth revealed.

According to the *Diagnostic and Statistical Manual of Mental Disorders*, known in the trade as the *DSM*, schizophrenia is characterized by "bizarre delusions" and "hallucinations" and other factors that are present "at least one month." While schizophrenia may be due to a variety of factors, including the patient's home and environmental background, in Justin's case, there might also have been a genetic component.

By his senior year in high school, Justin had begun having the "bizarre delusions" the *DSM* cites. He was also having major problems in school. He couldn't seem to sit for very long and he had trouble paying attention in class. His family did not realize the road he was traveling down until one night, when Elizabeth came home from work.

That night when she got home, it was pitch black and cool, a full moon high in the sky. And there was Justin digging a hole on the front lawn. His red, white and blue skin shone under the moonlight. He had painted himself in Pace High School's patriotic colors using some sort of shiny paint from head to toe.

"Justin, why you diggin' that hole?" his mother asked him, perplexed.

Justin looked up with a bright smile.

"Mama, I'm digging a hole for a fallout shelter because the Germans are going to attack."

Justin was having a hallucination that he was back in the United States during World War II when blackouts were staged to get people ready in case there ever was a German invasion. Inside the house, Elizabeth found Justin's paint bottles empty. He had chosen to paint himself with the toxic paint that he usually used on his models of planes and ships.

Between the body painting and the delusion, Elizabeth wasn't sure what to do. It was Cory who realized the problem was beyond their capabilities and suggested she call an ambulance, which Elizabeth did. The responding EMTs took Justin to Sacred Heart Hospital in Pensacola, the same hospital where he had been born.

"Justin was laughing and carrying on like nothing had happened," Elizabeth recalled. "The doctors were afraid he was high on the paint fumes. Even when they took the paint off him, he was still so high; the doctors were afraid that when he came down, he'd have a massive heart attack. He kept acting weird."

Realizing that Justin needed a psychiatric workup, they called a police cruiser to escort him to First Steps, the mental-health facility where he would be tested and diagnosed. Despite the fact that Justin had never been violent, the cops put him in cuffs for transport. The cops figured he was a psychiatric patient; they didn't want to take any chances if he turned violent. They drove Justin out to First Steps, where the doctors ran all kinds of psychological and physical tests on him, trying to figure out why he seemed so high despite being "off" the paint fumes.

"Mama, I want to get out of here," Justin said to his mother after he'd been at First Steps for a few weeks.

It was a plaintive cry from her youngest child, but Elizabeth Livingston knew there was nothing she could do to get him discharged. The state had him. The state was the boss, Elizabeth felt. All she could do was get her son through it the best way she could.

"Justin, pretend you're at the Holiday Inn and you got all these people waiting on you. That's not so bad, right?"

"Mama, it's not the Holiday Inn! I can't get out!" Justin pleaded.

Elizabeth's heart broke for her son, but there was nothing they could do. She'd had enough tragedy in her life to know that sometimes you just have to let the string play itself out. While Justin was being evaluated, Felicia, his older sister, was having a baby at another hospital in the area. Adding to her stress level, Elizabeth's father was dying in a West Florida hospital. Every day after she finished her work as school custodian, she had to rush to three hospitals to see three relatives.

It took another two weeks after Justin's desperate plea, but at the thirty-day mark, the professionals at First Steps finally arrived at a diagnosis.

"They diagnosed Justin as suffering from attention deficit disorder (ADD) and schizophrenia.

They gave him medication for both things," said Elizabeth.

The ADD diagnosis accounted for Justin's problems in school. According to the *DSM*, ADD is characterized as a "persistent pattern of inattention and/or hyperactivity-impulsivity that is more frequent and severe than is typically observed in individuals at a comparable level of development."

Justin was lucky; he responded well to the medications. His delusions and hallucinations disappeared. He still had ADD but could focus better. His life, though, had been irretrievably changed. For the rest of his life, he would be subject to major emotional problems unless he took his medication. He took it diligently every night at seven o'clock. And through it all, his mother recalled, he never lost his bright smile.

Justin had endured five years of dental work and the braces had just come off in the winter of 1998. The dental work left him with an eye-grabbing white smile and a dental appliance that he secretly wore in the back of his mouth to finish off the straightening process. It was that bright smile that graced the photos Elizabeth decided to use to find her son. She gave copies to the Santa Rosa County Sheriff's Office.

"Justin was really a sweet lil' feller. He was all of six feet and weighed one hundred thirty-five pounds soaking wet. He was easy to get along with. Everybody liked Justin. He had this thing—ADD. It happened . . . when he became a teenager," she told the cops haltingly.

In most missing-persons cases, the missing person turns up unharmed. The Santa Rosa County Sheriff's Office therefore hoped they wouldn't have to use the photos. They would distribute copies to beat cops, knowing full well that it is only the small minority of missing-persons cases where things get more serious.

But Elizabeth Livingston already knew in her gut that things had gone to the next level. Justin was in trouble and she told that to the police adamantly. Otherwise he would have come home and taken his medication. The last thing Justin wanted was to go delusional again and get confined to First Steps.

After a few sleepless nights and no reports from the police, Elizabeth felt that she had to take things into her own hands. If she was going to find her son, she would have to do it herself. She gathered up the photos she had given the police and pasted them on eleven-by-sixteen poster board. There was Justin's 1997 Pace High School graduation photograph, in which he proudly holds the diploma that he worked so hard to get, his senior prom shot, a photograph of him and Felicia making funny faces, and his yearbook photo, complete with tux.

Elizabeth wrote this copy across the poster:

MISSING—ENDANGERED
Justin Kyle Livingston
D.O.B. Feb. 23, 1978, missing since April 9, 1998, 7 PM.
6ft tall—135 lbs.
Black Hair/Brown Eyes
Tall/Thin/Always Smiling

Last Seen By: Roy lee, Jon & Ricky Lawrence, & Jeremiah
Rodgers on West Spencer Field Road (Pace)

Looking at his graduation picture, Elizabeth
remembered that Justin had required special tu-
toring, which necessitated transporting him to
another school in the county.

"Justin was taking some special courses up at
Laughlin and he'd get picked up by this bus. The
initials on the side were SLD. Justin said [kidding]
that was for 'slow-learning dummies,'" Elizabeth related, laughing at the memory.

Traveling up to the Wal-Mart on Route 90, Elizabeth made copies of the poster and distributed
them to friends and family. They scattered around
town, posting them wherever they could. Elizabeth
had already been to four locations around Pace
herself when she arrived at the Corner Store. It was
a convenience store a few blocks up from her
home. Inside, an attractive red-haired girl was behind the register. The girl had only recently started
there. Elizabeth seemed to recall that she was related to the man who owned the store.

"I'd like to post this outside if I could," said Elizabeth, holding the copy of the poster.

"Sure," said the girl behind the counter. "No
problem."

"Thank you," said Elizabeth politely. "You went to
Pace too, right?"

"I still am. Graduating this semester," said the girl
brightly. "I'm Jenny Robinson," she said, extending
her hand in greeting.

Elizabeth shook hands.

"My son, Justin, graduated in 1997. Do you know him?"

The girl said she didn't. Outside, Elizabeth stapled Justin's poster to a utility pole. She looked at the picture of her son laughing with her daughter and making those funny faces and remembered the day he died temporarily. It had been a long time ago.

"When Justin was two and a half, he had to have a kidney removed. It was when a hurricane came through," said Ms. Livingston, speaking in a Deep South drawl that made "hurricane" sound like "her-rican."

What happened was that Justin had a fever that spiked at 106 degrees. Touching his hot skin, Elizabeth realized something was wrong; her baby wasn't breathing. He had flat-lined. The ambulance had already been called but was delayed because of the wailing wind and heavy sheets of wind the hurricane was throwing down from the heavens. There was no time to wait.

Elizabeth Livingston had some training in CPR and so she began massaging her son's chest. She made sure that her downward strokes on his little baby chest were not enough to fracture a rib, but concentrated simply on getting the heart working. By the time the EMTs arrived, little Justin was breathing on his own again, thanks to his mother's heroic efforts.

After being rushed in an ambulance to the hospital, the doctors ran all kinds of tests on Justin. They came to the conclusion that one of Justin's kidneys was not functioning properly. He needed a nephrectomy, or kidney removal. Without such a procedure, the kidney would continue to malfunction, pouring toxins into the body. Justin would die and this time there would be no bringing him back.

"They said he had something strange in his urine," Elizabeth recalled. She agreed to the operation; it was performed; Justin survived. Now Elizabeth could only hope he was still alive. She finished tacking up the poster.

A week later, in the middle of April, the police still had no leads and Justin had not come home. Elizabeth was trying to get her mind off her worries and was outside weeding her garden. She looked up from some chickweed to see Jeremiah Rodgers and Jon Lawrence stride up to the fence that ringed her home.

"You gotta take our names off that poster," Lawrence complained.

"Yeah," Rodgers added, "you got no right to put our names out there on that there poster. We want you to take our names off now."

Elizabeth found their request rather strange.

"There was some kind of strange vibe about them. Everyone else whose name was on the poster understood and was cooperative, but those two, they were downright rude."

She told them that she was just trying to find her son, that she was terribly worried about him. They didn't want to hear it. Once again, they insisted she take their names off her posters.

"Get away," she said curtly.

Not waiting, she went into the house and slammed the door. *Oh, Lord,* she thought, *a Lawrence is involved with my baby's disappearance. Something has happened to Justin. I'm sure of it now.*

"I suspected everyone," Elizabeth said later. "I've had to go through a lot of murder in my family. Seven, in fact—seven family members been murdered. It's our family curse. Justin's daddy himself was murdered ten years ago."

Elizabeth had been in the process of divorcing her husband, Jimmie, the decade before. She was already separated from him at the time but had to go see him about something. She took a friend, Jeff Hunter, along for protection because Jimmie could be unstable. Sure enough, Jimmie started an argument and the two men fought. When it was over, Jimmie Livingston lay dead on the pavement, stabbed to death.

Elizabeth was determined that the "family curse" not befall Justin. But the fact that Justin was last seen with the Lawrence family worried her considerably. Elizabeth and the Lawrences were blood kin, but that did not distort her view of them. She knew that being related biologically to somebody didn't make them a better human being.

"My mother on her deathbed, she told me never to have anything to do with the Lawrences," recalled Elizabeth Livingston. "I am related through my first cousin's son. My mother was a Lawrence. Her brother's son's son."

* * *

Elizabeth Livingston had been correct in taking the responsibility for her son's search effort into her own hands.

No detective had been actively working the case. It was not a priority for the simple reason there was no indication of foul play. There was no crime scene to look at for answers. Cursory questions of his acquaintances had shown nothing. No one knew where he was.

As for Rodgers and Lawrence, they had not yet been questioned extensively. There were certainly better suspects in Pace and Milton, men who had been tried and convicted of violent crimes who had served time and were now out on the street. Why should anyone suspect two former mental patients without any history of violent crime?

It would take a really good cop to put it together.

CHAPTER 3

1997

Michael Keaton and Todd Hand were kidding around on the set of *Desperate Measures*. Hand was the thirty-seven-year-old director of security for the film in which Keaton played a killer who just happened to be a bone marrow donor for a cop's critically ill young son. For Keaton, playing a killer for only the second time in his career, it turned out to be a colossal flop. It was one in a string of disappointing films he did after playing Batman. For Todd Hand, the film represented the end of his personal three-year Pennsylvania odyssey.

Hand had been traveling aimlessly since he divorced his wife three years before in Florida. He followed her north after their divorce because she had custody of their child and moved back to Pennsylvania. Hand came from central Pennsylvania; he had only immigrated to Florida after his graduation from Penn State with a B.S. in criminal justice. Once in the Sunshine State, he had pursued a career in law enforcement, rising to become a detective in Polk County. He gave up all that to be near his child.

The problem was, being a cop wasn't just his vocation, it was his avocation. He just loved it. It wasn't surprising, then, that he drifted through a series of dead-end jobs. His heart wasn't in any of them. Finally he got work in private security. The hospital set in *Desperate Measures* was actually a downtown building in Pittsburgh that the producers dressed up to look like the film's San Francisco hospital setting. Most of the shooting took place at night.

One night after he had kibitzed with the affable Keaton between takes, Hand went back, alone, to his office. He sat there in the darkness and wondered where his life was going. Like his acting friend's alter ego Bruce Wayne, Hand had some personal problems that needed sorting out.

Hand could have stayed in private security. He enjoyed schmoozing with Keaton and his costar Andy Garcia. Considering the difficulty of the case about to come his way, he probably should have stayed. However, he couldn't get being a cop out of his blood. So, he decided that his daughter had matured enough that he could tend to one of his own needs.

Looking at a map of Florida, he literally picked Santa Rosa County out at random. He thought it might be a good place to work. After *Desperate Measures* wrapped, he packed up his car with everything he owned and drove south. He figured it wouldn't take him long to rise through the ranks from street officer to detective.

* * *

April 16, 1998, Milton, Florida

Santa Rosa was only too happy to hire Hand as a deputy on patrol. Hand figured that considering his experience, it wouldn't be long until he made detective. He was right. In six short months, he was promoted to the detective bureau, hung up his uniform and put on a sports jacket and slacks.

It was Todd Hand's first day at his new job as detective. He strode purposefully into the detective bureau of the Santa Rosa County Sheriff's Office in Milton, Florida, and reported in to his lieutenant, Josh Randall. Randall was getting a good man. Hand had a total of fifteen years of experience as a cop.

In the squad room after his meeting with the lieutenant, Hand looked around. The place was narrow and cramped and smelled of mildew. Everything in Santa Rosa County smelled from mildew. Not only did the Blackwater River cut right across it, the county itself had a southern border on the Gulf of Mexico, from whence mighty storms rolled in during hurricane season in the fall.

"You can use this desk over here," said Joe McCurdy. McCurdy was a detective with a big ol' country boy demeanor. He led Hand to a battered wooden desk. Hand sat down and McCurdy came back with a folder.

"Here you go." McCurdy placed the folder on the desk in front of Hand. "You can take care of this one. Welcome to the Santa Rosa County Detective Bureau." Hand looked at the folder. Written in bold letters on the front was the name Justin Livingston. Hand opened it and began reading:

"10 April, 1998. The complainant, Elizabeth Livingston, stated that her son, Justin Livingston, didn't come home last night or this morning. The complainant stated she had last seen her son at 10:00 AM on 04-09-98. At that time, he was lying in bed at his residence. The complainant didn't know what her son was wearing when he left the residence."

So far, nothing out of the ordinary. The report continued:

"The complainant stated that her son was mentally disabled. He takes medication for paranoid schizophrenic [sic]. The complainant stated that Justin has missed three doses of his medication. If he doesn't receive his medication, he becomes very paranoid. After becoming paranoid and depressed, he makes attempts to harm himself."

Great, thought Hand. *Not only is this kid mentally disabled, he's suicidal and paranoid when he's not on his "meds."*

"For all I knew, this kid had found some girl, gone down to [the nearby party town] of Fort Walton and was having a good old time," Hand later said.

Hand knew that over the years, research in criminal justice has found that over 80 percent of missing-persons cases are solved successfully—that is, the missing person shows up on his own, unharmed. That leaves 20 percent unaccounted for, meaning those people are in trouble. It is within this latter group that Todd Hand sincerely hoped Justin Livingston had not fallen into. Chances were that Justin Livingston would eventually show up alive and well.

If Justin fell into the 20 percent grouping, the first twenty-four hours he was missing were all important. If he was abducted but alive, it was during that period of time the cops had the best shot of catching up with him because the trail was warm. After that, it diminished to the point of cold freeze, which was exactly where Todd Hand was picking it up. Hand opened the file again.

"According to the complainant, Justin wasn't depressed or upset about anything. The complainant stated that Justin hangs out at two different residences in the area. These locations were check [*sic*] with negative results." The investigating officers Reed and Malloy got a statement from the mother in which she said that Justin went walking off in the afternoon. She didn't know where he went. He just never came home. That was the last she'd seen of him.

Even in this age of forensic magic, cops still rely on their knowledge of the territory they patrol, their beat, to solve crimes. In Santa Rosa County, Hand was confronted with a society that locals had affectionately nicknamed Lower Alabama or the Redneck Riviera. The smarter locals knew that meant that quite a few of their neighbors were rather backward country folk who had yet to make the evolutionary climb into the twenty-first century. Such snide observations aside, Hand had the immediate obstacle that he wasn't a local. He knew nothing of the kinds of local social mores that a smart cop relies on to solve cases. Milton was a new beat. He'd have to pick up on the way people acted, what was considered normal versus suspicious.

Hand drove out to see Elizabeth Livingston in an unmarked gray '96 Mercury Sable. He found her in her trailer, still fretting. It was three days after Justin had disappeared.

"Did you do anything?" Hand asked.

"Like what?"

"An argument?"

She answered no.

"Does he have any enemies?"

Again a no.

While they were chatting, Livingston heard brakes squealing outside her trailer, up the driveway across the street. She convinced Hand to run over and look for tire marks, signs of anything wrong. Maybe Justin had been hit with a car and was lying dead someplace.

"She told me that the night Justin didn't show up, the guy who lived in the house across the street had a big fire going. Justin stopped there earlier before he went to Jon Lawrence's home," Hand later said.

The fire, it turned out, was nothing—just the neighbor burning some leaves. Another neighbor, Lincoln Hayes, had been involved in a drowning death in Los Angeles, but he was in the Everglades when Justin disappeared and his whereabouts were accounted for. What complicated the investigation further was that Justin's apparent normality meant that no one gave him a second look.

Hand's investigation would later show that Justin "had the mental capacity of a twelve-year-old. He was very immature, even for a twelve-year-old." Hand questioned the neighbors, looking for the last people that saw Justin in the neighborhood. It took a while, but finally he came across a neighbor, Jim Kelly, who had seen something.

"I saw a guy in a pickup truck let Justin out early in the afternoon," Kelly told Hand. "Justin went into his trailer, came out, got back into the pickup and the guy drove off."

When she heard the truck's description, neighbor Leslie Shepard said it matched the one driven by Ricky Lawrence. He lived with his brother Jonathan a few streets over. Hand hit the Merc's gas and tooled over to what the cops would come to describe derisively as "the Lawrence compound."

The Lawrence compound was three run-down buildings on a one-acre square of suburban property in a lower-middle-class neighborhood in Milton. It was set off from the street, with access by a narrow, weed-strewn driveway. A bolted-up cattle gate blocked the entrance. Without a warrant, Hand couldn't proceed any farther.

Hand checked with some other neighbors. They told him that Ricky Lawrence worked for the Delgaudio Wood Chipping Company in town; Hand called him there.

"I'm trying to find Justin Livingston," Hand told Ricky Lawrence over the phone.

Ricky replied that he was working on his truck the day Justin disappeared. Justin came over in the afternoon. For some reason, he was all duded up in snakeskin cowboy boots, a Levi's green-striped cowboy shirt and Levi's boot jeans. Justin usually dressed casually. Seeing him all dressed up was unusual.

Despite his fancy outfit, Justin helped Ricky do some mechanical work on the truck. When Ricky was satisfied, he closed the hood and took it for a test drive. Justin came along and told Ricky about a tape that he wanted him to listen to. That's when Ricky drove him over to his trailer. Almost instantly, Justin was in and out of his trailer with the tape and Ricky drove off.

So far, Hand wasn't surprised. Until that afternoon, Justin Livingston had been alive and well—and well dressed at that, if you liked cowboy dress.

After picking up the tape, Ricky claimed that he drove back to the Lawrence compound. He and Justin hung around for a while until Jonathan Lawrence and his friend Jeremiah Rodgers showed up, along with Uncle Roy, who lived in a bus on the property. Then Justin drove off with Rodgers and Lawrence.

"That was the last time I saw Justin," Ricky told Hand.

Back at the office, he called Jonathan Lawrence. He got his answering machine and left a message. Lawrence called him back quickly.

"Me and Jeremiah drove off with Justin, and then

went back to the Airstream to watch a movie, *The Shining*," Lawrence told Hand.

That's the film based on the Stephen King novel of the same name where Jack Nicholson plays a homicidal maniac named John, who, in the film's penultimate moment, axes a door down to kill his wife, after which he sticks his head through the splintered door and announces with glee, "Heeere's Johnny."

Lawrence liked that scene because his name was Jon too, albeit spelled differently. But he identified with Nicholson's raging homicidal maniac.

"Justin really wanted to watch it," Lawrence continued. "Jeremiah had a little marijuana, so we smoked together. Justin was a weedhead."

When the movie was over, Justin got up, Lawrence claimed.

"Me and Jeremiah said we was gonna take a ride. Justin, he said he was going down to the video store to get a video."

Lawrence said he watched as Justin walked down the block, toward the highway where the video store was located. That was the last he saw of him.

"What's Rodgers's number?" Hand asked ~~Justin~~ Jon, who promptly offered him Lisa Johnson's number. Lisa was Rodgers's girlfriend. "They lived together," Lawrence later said.

"I remember that on Justin's twentieth birthday, he had gone to services with me and he raised his hand that day in church to say something. The theme of that day's service was 'Staying Alive,' Elizabeth Livingston recalled.

She fell back on her faith now to sustain her in her search for Justin. Elizabeth needed to; she was falling apart. She expected the worst, though didn't want to admit it.

Todd Hand intended to interview Jonathan Lawrence in person later, but for now, his primary task was to account for Justin's movements. If he could do that, he thought, he could track him down.

Hand called Lisa Johnson's, got a machine, identified himself and left a message for Rodgers to call him. That done, he drove over to the video store that Lawrence said Justin had been going to when he disappeared. The place was called Alternate Video. It not only stocked the usual Hollywood movies, it had special sections devoted to well-known directors and film genres. Its manager, Ike Clayton, said that the Livingstons had an account with them, but neither Justin nor his mother had rented videos for a while.

Hand had Clayton pull the surveillance tape from the store security camera. Justin wasn't on it. Hand spoke to the two counter people who were working the night Justin disappeared. He described the young man carefully. Neither could recall Justin being there.

Hand called Rodgers and Lawrence again and left messages to call him back. Lawrence would later call him back, but not his friend.

That pissed Todd Hand off. Though there really was no reason yet to suspect that anything had happened to Justin, Hand decided to hit the Florida law enforcement on-line database at the sheriff's office. Here's what came up on Rodgers:

Name: JEREMIAH MARTEL RODGERS

Race: CAUCASIAN

Sex: MALE

Hair Color: BROWN

Eye Color: BROWN

Height: 5'07"

Weight: 179

Birth Date: 04/19/1977

Aliases: JEREMIAH RODGERS, JEREMIAH M. RODGERS, JEREMIAH MARTEL RODGERS

Identifiers: FINGERPRINT CLASS—22PIPO1718POPIPI14

Scars, Marks and Tattoos: HEAD ("X"), LEFT ANKLE ("ROSE"), RIGHT HAND ("FIRE-CRACKER")

Prior Prison History: (Note: Data reflected covers periods of incarceration with the Florida Dept. of Corrections since January of 1983):

ARRESTED GRAND THEFT AUTO,

5/19/1993, SENTENCED 8/16/1993, LAKE COUNTY, PRISON SENTENCE LENGTH, 4 Y 6M 0D [PART OF SENTENCED SERVED AT CHATTAHOOCHEE]

Lawrence's file wasn't much different:

Name: JONATHAN H. LAWRENCE

Race: CAUCASIAN

Sex: MALE

Hair Color: RED OR AUBURN

Eye Color: BROWN

Height: 5'07"

Weight: 166

Birth Date: 04/12/1975

Aliases: JON LAWRENCE, JONATHAN LAWRENCE, JONATHAN HUEY LAWRENCE, JONATHAN LAWRENCE, JONATHAN H. LAWRENCE

Identifiers: FINGERPRINT CLASS— POPIPIPIPIPIPIPIPIPI

Scars, Marks and Tattoos: BOTH WRISTS

Prior Prison History: (Note: Data reflected covers periods of incarceration with the Florida Dept.of Corrections since January of 1983)

ARRESTED CRIMINAL MISCHIEF/PROP.

DAMAGE, 05/18/1993, SANTA ROSE
COUNTY, SENTENCED 11/02/1993,
PRISON SENTENCE LENGTH, 4Y 0M 0D
[PART OF SENTENCE SERVED AT CHAT-
TAHOOCHE]

Chattahoochee was the state's once-notorious
mental hospital. *Holy shit, what a bunch of nuts around
here,* Hand thought. Since they had been in different
prisons before being transferred to Chattahoochee,
Hand figured they had met up there. Noting
Lawrence's mental history, Hand reasoned that the
wrist scars might be from suicide attempts. He
wouldn't know until he looked at Lawrence in short
sleeves. Yet, despite their records, there was still no
indication of foul play.

"Rodgers and Lawrence and their checkered past
was interesting to me," said Hand later. "Their record
of crimes and record of confinement in a mental
hospital made them *damn* interesting. And that's
when the Justin Livingston sightings started happening." Hand later explained.

Cops started funneling him lead sheets, reports
from locals who claimed to have seen Justin standing
on a street corner, at a local bar, or hiding out on the
streets to get away from his mom. None of the leads
checked out. Hand began to realize that in the Milton community everyone wanted to help, but in their
zeal to do so, people overreacted.

Because Hand wasn't a local, he didn't know that
such "helpful" sightings were not uncommon from
the country folk who populated the area. And then,

there was this one anonymous caller. The fellow called and left a message on Hand's phone.

"I just seen Justin in Fort Walton Beach with a girl," said the caller.

There was something about the message that didn't sound right to Hand. Unfortunately, he neglected to save it. But it gnawed at him.

"Then just when I start to suspect those two assholes, I get a report from somebody again who says he saw Justin. And another in the second or third week I'm working on the case from a minister's son. He swore up and down he'd seen Justin," Hand related.

But all the sightings were dead ends. By the end of the month, Justin still hadn't shown up. Finally Hand got Jeremiah Rodgers on the phone.

"He was kind of squirrelly with me. Not real helpful, but definitely not rude. He was real smooth and very soft-spoken. I felt something when I talked to him." he later recounted.

"Why don't you come in and talk with me?'" Hand asked him.

"Okay, I'll come over," Rodgers replied.

They made an appointment, but at the last minute, Rodgers called and said he couldn't make it. A few days later, Rodgers called back.

Saturday, April 18, 1998

"When was the last time you saw Justin Livingston?" Hand asked over the phone.

Rodgers answered that he last saw Justin on Thursday, April 9, walking southbound on West Spencer Field Road at approximately 2:30 P.M. He figured Livingston was walking down to find cigarettes and pick up a rental at the video store.

Rodgers said that sometime in the middle of the afternoon, he had gone over to Lawrence's trailer home. He socialized with Lawrence, Rick and their uncle Roy while Rick and Roy were repairing Rick's truck. Sometime during that period, Justin arrived on foot. He hung around, joked and acted stupid, like he usually did. Justin spent the rest of the afternoon bumming cigarettes from him. He gave Hand the same story about watching *The Shining*, with the added detail that Livingston left during the climactic scene in the film involving the maze. He said good-bye and left to go rent a video.

Up until that last detail about *The Shining*, Rodgers had been consistent with Lawrence's version of what had happened. It certainly was plausible. But what fan goes out of his way to see a movie only to walk away before the climax, especially one with as bloody and dramatic an ending as *The Shining*?

"I liked Justin," said Rodgers. "Justin'd walk around the neighborhood all the time. He would bum cigarettes, food, beer and weed from everybody on a regular basis."

"Do you think he was in danger?"

"No." Rodgers added that he had no idea where Justin might be.

"Did he have any cash on him?"

Hand needed to rule out robbery conclusively.

"I don't know if he did or not. Justin received money for some type of disability from the government."

He told him to call back if he had any additional information.

April 22, 1998

Hand picked up the ringing telephone. Justin Livingston's mother, Elizabeth, was on the other end of the line. Like most mothers with missing children, she was anxious, calling at least once a day to see if any progress was being made in tracking her baby down.

"I'm talking to her at least once a day on the phone, usually twice. What I have learned over the years is that mothers have an especially strong intuition about their sons and you have to listen to that intuition. She may be goofy, but she had that feeling that something happened to him. He would never just disappear like that."

Elizabeth told Hand that there was a bad smell up the road from her house. "I got ahold of Lucas McCain. He has a bloodhound from the Jimmy Ryce Center."

Jimmy Ryce was a nine-year-old boy who was kidnapped at gunpoint, raped and murdered on September 11, 1995. The Jimmy Ryce Center for Victims of Predatory Abduction was established in his memory. Among other functions, the organization provides bloodhounds—what cops call cadaver dogs—free to law enforcement to find abducted and lost children.

That was how, in late April, Lucas McCain showed up with his bloodhound, Mark. Hand filled McCain in on the case and the dog was let go in the neighborhood to see if he could pick up Justin's scent. But the dog found nothing in Justin's neighborhood. On a hunch, Hand suggested they go to the Lawrence compound and try the dog over there. They drove over and parked in the driveway. Rick Lawrence was home.

"Ricky, do you mind if I run the bloodhound around the property," Hand asked.

"No problem," Ricky answered.

McCain took the dog off the leash and it went running. While McCain was taking care of that, Hand was standing on the drive chatting with Ricky and Uncle Roy when a red sports car with two people in it drove up. In the passenger seat was a guy with his shirt off.

The man looked to be in his early twenties. He was short, with a bright smile. When he got out of the car, Hand saw that he was well built, just like a guy who had been hitting the weights in prison. His body, covered in tattoos, seemed to confirm that hypothesis.

As for the woman who drove, "she looked like the cover girl on a poison bottle," Hand later said about the woman. "She looked like so many females in Santa Rosa County—no chin and bulbous stomach."

The man put his shirt back on and Ricky introduced Hand to Jeremiah Rodgers and his girlfriend,

Lisa Johnson. Everyone shook hands like they were meeting at a party instead of in the middle of a missing-persons investigation. Hand thought to himself that it was luck he was driving an unmarked car. Had Rodgers seen a marked cruiser as he drove in, he could easily have driven right back out.

"You know, Justin might be in Florida town at Jack's. Jack's a homosexual who had furnished weed and rush to Justin in exchange for some type of sexual favors," Rodgers volunteered.

That's a new one, Hand thought. *He's implying that Justin was in some sort of strange homosexual/drug deal that caused his death.* Lisa said very little but supported Rodgers's version of events by physical head nodding and occasional "yeahs."

"I liked Worm," Rodgers added, "and I'm concerned about him."

After about fifteen or twenty minutes spent scouring the property, the dog began to paw at the earth. It was digging a hole down, down. . . . There was a small skeleton. McCain put the dog back on its leash as Hand bent down to check out the discovery.

It was a skeleton, all right, of a bird, which somebody had buried. The closest Hand could come to seeing that any crime was committed on the property was a cursory search of the house that yielded a little marijuana plant growing in a pot.

"Ricky," Hand called.

Ricky came over.

"Get rid of it," Hand ordered. "I'm not going to do anything about it."

The possession of that plant was a misdemeanor.

The last thing a good cop would do in a situation like this is arrest somebody for a misdemeanor when he might be helpful later on in prosecuting a felony.

"Just get rid of it," Hand repeated.

As he got back into his car, Hand took another look at Lisa. *He's using her,* Hand thought.

"She could never get anybody as good-looking as Rodgers. The only reason Rodgers was with her was because he was using her. He'd pork her because he had no place to live and she was stupid enough to let him," Hand later said.

As he drove out of the compound, Hand said good-bye to Rodgers, who smiled and shouted, "see ya." Later, back at the office, Hand thought about the anonymous message he had erased weeks before.

"I could have sworn it was Jeremiah Rodgers's voice on the tape I didn't keep. That fucker called me and left that anonymous message."

Back upstairs, Hand looked again at Lawrence's file. There was a notation about him having an uncle, Gary Lawrence. Gary was Lawrence's father's baby brother. Hand went on-line and visited the Florida State Prisons site. Once there, Hand typed in Gary Lawrence's name. This is what came up:

Name: GARY LAWRENCE

Race: CAUCASIAN

Sex: MALE

Hair Color: BLONDE OR STRAWBERRY

Eye Color: BLUE

Height: 6'0"

Weight: 190

Birth Date: 06/29/1957

Initial Receipt Date: 02/21/1991

Current Facility: UNION C. I.

Current Classification Status: DEATH ROW

Current Custody: MAXIMUM, DEATH SEN-
TENCE

Aliases: GARY LAWRENCE

Identifiers: FINGERPRINT CLASS—
POPI15PO19130914CI16

Scars, Marks, and Tattoos: STOMACH SCAR,
LONG AND VERTICAL FROM SURGERY;
TATTOOS ON FACE, DOT ON LEFT CHEEK
AND TIME MARK ON RIGHT CHEEK; AX
GOING THROUGH SKULL HEAD ON LEFT
ARM; HEART ON LEFT CHEST; HARLEY
WINGS ON LEFT SHOUDLER; BRACELET
OR CHAIN ON RIGHT ARM; DAGGER
GOING THROUGH STAR ON RIGHT ARM;
SURFER CROSS ON RIGHT ARM

There followed a long criminal record stretching
back two decades. That helped to explain why he
was covered in tattoos. Prison culture encourages
festooning the body with those decorations. At one
time or another, Gary Lawrence had been arrested
and convicted of numerous offenses, including

burglary and grand-theft firearm. He had been paroled for those offenses and had to report in every week to his parole officer.

He committed first-degree murder, commission of felony, on July 22, 1994. Sentenced on May 5, 1995, he was condemned to die. The judge also tacked on convictions for conspiracy to commit murder and grand-theft motor vehicle, with concurrent five-year sentences. Reading farther, Hand saw earlier convictions on a variety of criminal charges for which he served ten more years behind bars.

Hand finished reading. Jon Lawrence was the nephew of a murderer on Florida's death row, with a record as long as the proverbial arm. Could the apple fall far from the tree?

Hand knew that in Florida, death meant death. Unlike some other states that have the death penalty on the books and never use it, Florida did so frequently. Few murderers had their sentences overturned or commuted on appeal. Most were "fried" in the state's electric chair.

CHAPTER 4

May 7, 1998

Eighteen-year-old Jennifer Robinson lived in a small tract house in Pace, with her mother, Diane Robinson, and Diane's boyfriend, Dennis Randall.

When Jenny Robinson woke up in her bedroom that day, she was staring Elvis Presley right in the face. It made no difference that "the King" had died two decades before. In Jenny's small bedroom, the King lived. On the wall directly across from her single bed was a giant four-by-four poster of Elvis. This wasn't the portly prince of pop from the late 1970s, but the earlier Elvis, *the real Elvis* as Jenny often thought.

There he was, posing above her dresser, circa 1960, dressed in black jacket and black pants, black vest, black bow tie, posed against a foreground of stuffed animals. The stuffed animals were on the dresser and their heads obscured part of Elvis's white shirt.

Her cat, Sidewinder, shoved its paw around on the floor, cluttered with school work. There were tons of paperwork and books and reports covering every exposed surface, including the desk in the corner, where Jenny did her homework. The papers and books competed for space with Elvis CDs and eight or nine videos of Elvis's films. Jenny thought his 1950s films were vastly superior to the stuff he churned out in the '60s.

When she got up that day, she was excited. Today was the day she had her date with Jeremiah Rodgers. He was this good-looking guy she met down at the convenience store where she worked. She looked over at her desk. There, sitting on her homework, was her graduation yearbook. She had gotten it just a few days before, in time to bring it to graduation and get all of her friends to sign it. They would bring their copies to graduation, the last time they would all be together.

She got up and padded across the room. As she had so many times since she had gotten it, Jenny opened the book and leafed through it. It was the usual collection of sophomoric humor and false nostalgia of kids who suddenly realize the world is never going to be quite the same safe place again.

In the yearbook, the pictures of the graduating seniors are the only ones in color. Placed in the "well," or center of the book, Jenny's was on page 93, top row, second from right. There she was, her head tilted to the left as the photographer had ordered, the head tilt offering a question to the future. Jenny Robinson hadn't been the most popular girl in high school, or the least. She wasn't a great athlete or student, but she had the purest red hair. It was unique in its hue and vibrancy. Coupling that with her outgoing personality and zaftig figure, she was found attractive by boys. It was a specific part of that zaftig figure that Jonathan Lawrence would later fantasize about.

Across town at the Lawrence compound, Jonathan Lawrence woke up in his grungy bedroom. He had all kinds of stuff scattered about. There was the white supremacist literature, the books about devil worship and the application to join one of the country's biggest devil worshiping groups. On his nightstand was a book Lawrence read faithfully called *The Incredible Machine*. He picked it up to read.

An anatomy book, *The Incredible Machine* had numerous diagrams of the human body. Lawrence paged through it, noticing the sections that he'd marked in ink, including a picture of a female body. He had circled the calf muscle on one leg of the body in the diagram and looked at it longingly. Eventually he put the book down and got dressed in jeans and a T-shirt. On the way to the door, he passed by his footlocker, where he kept his real treasures.

Inside was *Serial Killers* from Time-Life Books. It contained pictorial essays on serial killers, whom Lawrence admired: Ted Bundy, John Wayne Gacy, David "Son of Sam" Berkowitz and Dennis Nielsen. He also had two books about snipers: Major John L. Plaster's *The Ultimate Sniper: An Advanced Training Manual for Military Police Snipers* and J. David Truby's *Silencers, Snipers and Assassins: An Overview of Whispering Death.*

Elsewhere in the trunk was a battered faux-leather scrapbook that included his GED certificate, karate certificate, numerous articles on the Ku Klux Klan and, of course, serial killers. Perhaps his most valuable possession was the certification of his "citizenship" in the American Knights of the Ku Klux Klan, dated February 23, 1998.

That morning when he left his house, Jon Lawrence was bound for the sheriff's department, where he was supposed to take some sort of test that Todd Hand had set up. Hand was already there, waiting for him to arrive. During the month that Hand had been on the Livingston disappearance, no hard evidence had turned up to indicate where Justin was or, indeed, if he was still alive. Hand casually called Rodgers and Lawrence separately. Each time, he went over their story. Each time, they stuck to it: they were watching *The Shining* and then Justin walked off before the bloody climax.

Hand knew the movie. He had seen it; he just couldn't believe Justin would walk away before Jack Nicholson got to do his thing at the end. Plus the tape story itself just sounded too convenient. Add that to their squirrelly backgrounds and the sum total was a firm belief that if Rodgers and Lawrence were not directly responsible for Justin's disappearance, they were certainly involved and knew more than they were telling.

The weak link of the two appeared to be Lawrence. While Jeremiah Rodgers never volunteered information and remained aloof, Jonathan Lawrence seemed eager to please. Playing on this,

Hand managed to convince Lawrence to voluntarily come in for a voice stress analysis.

"Jon, if you do this, it'll help us eliminate you once and for all as a suspect," he told Lawrence, who not only acquiesced, but had no fear that he might fail the test.

Voice stress analysis is a more accurate way than a conventional lie detector in telling whether or not a suspect, under questioning, is telling the truth. According to Paul Dennis at the Voice Stress Analysis Web site, "all muscles in the body, including the vocal cords, vibrate in the eight-to-twelve-Hz range. This is considered a feedback loop, similar to a thermostat/heater."

If the temperature goes too high or low, the body adjusts accordingly to bring it back within normal range.

Just as the temperature swings up and down over time, so too do the muscles tighten and loosen as they seek to maintain a constant tension. This is known to be caused by the production and release of a chemical, as explained in the *Scientific American* article "Psychological Tremor," Volume 224, Number 3, 1971. "In moments of stress, like when you tell a lie that you dare not get caught at, the body prepares for fight or flight by increasing the readiness of its muscles to spring into action," Dennis explained. Their vibration increases from the relaxed eight to nine Hz, to the stressed eleven-to-twelve-Hz range.

That was the key. Vibrations in the eleven-to-twelve-Hz range meant the subject was lying. Hand stood in the observation room. Through the two-way glass, he watched Lawrence undergoing the voice stress analysis. The ex-con was seated in a plain green interview room. His only company was Harman Newman, the analyst, who stood before the machine, asking questions and watching the readout.

During a break in the examination, Hand went in to talk to his suspect. He asked casual questions, designed to relax Lawrence and get him to trust him.

"How'd you get down here for the interview?" Hand asked casually.

"My mother drove me," Lawrence answered.

That would be interesting, to meet Jon Lawrence's mother, Hand thought.

Separated from the rest of the community by a long back road, the Santa Rosa County Police Department is a sprawling complex distinguished by a low-lying white brick building that houses, among other things, the detective bureau and forensic section. In the building's outer lobby, Hand found a woman seated alone on a scratched plastic chair. Her right leg was unusually straight. A cane lounged against the chair's back.

"Hi, I'm Todd Hand," he said.

He explained who he was, while his brown eyes went to the cane by her side, then down to her right leg, which looked withered.

"What happened to your leg?" he asked sympathetically.

"I got a staph infection," Iona Lawrence answered. "It worsened upon hospitalization. I can't even bend it now."

She quickly changed the subject from her leg to her son.

"I want to tell you what a good person my son is. When my leg was really bad, Jon waited on me hand and foot. He came by to feed me, to help me get around," she said, obviously proud of her son. Then she confided that her other son Wesley put a shotgun to his head at a party. It went off accidentally and killed him. The incident affected Jon quite a bit. Hand planned to look into that later.

He went back to look at Jonathan Lawrence, who was just finishing up the voice polygraph. Afterward, he told Lawrence, "I'll review the results and call you, okay?" Hand went to consult with Harman Newman, the voice stress analyst.

"Every time I asked him something specific about Justin Livingston's disappearance, his answer was a lie," Newman told him promptly.

In other words, Jon Lawrence, despite his mother's assurances to the contrary, was a liar. He knew something about Justin's disappearance, all right, which only made things that much more frustrating. Without hard evidence, there was nothing Hand could do to move on Lawrence and Rodgers. Without more evidence, he could never get a warrant to search the Lawrence home, where he felt certain he would find something implicating him. It was a legal conundrum.

By 4:00 P.M., at the end of his shift, Hand had found nothing new. He left, hopeful he might come up with something new tomorrow. But while

Hand's day was ending, for Rodgers and Lawrence, theirs was just beginning.

"There's this little convenience store [the Corner Store] a few blocks from our house. Jenny's uncle by marriage managed it. She filled out an application and he hired her as a stocker," recalled Diane Robinson.

For four to five hours every day after school, five days a week, Jenny came into the convenience store to stock the shelves. It was a safe job, her mother thought. She was working for a family member a few blocks away and Jenny's aunt even popped in every now and then to see how she was doing. Other people stopped in too.

"That's how she met Rodgers," continued Diane. "For three weeks, Rodgers kept coming in and asked Jenny to go out. She was a little unsure; he kept pursuing her.

"Jenny really didn't have much experience with guys," her mother recalled. "She dated some, but not often. There had been a special boyfriend she had for a while, but Jenny was redheaded and hot-tempered. When the boy called at eleven one night, she told him, 'You don't call my house at this time!' and that was that."

For a full week before Rodgers took Jenny out, he had been bragging to his brother, Elijah Waldrop, and anyone else who would listen, "about this new girl that works at the Corner Store." Rodgers never mentioned her name, but Elijah knew her by her nickname around school.

"Everybody called her 'Red,'" Waldrop stated in court documents. "She dated four or five of my friends," Elijah recalled.

At five feet three and a half inches and 145 pounds, Jenny "was a little chunky," according to her mother. She had a pretty, round face, framed by a mass of flowing reddish blond hair. She concentrated more on her studies and her extracurricular activities than anything else. An inveterate animal lover, from the ages of nine to eleven, she had volunteered at a nearby animal shelter every afternoon. She had a mean old cat named Sidewinder, which she loved dearly.

Rodgers told her nothing of his criminal background or his "relationship" with Lisa Johnson. He made it seem like he was just any other working-class single guy. No matter her previous experience with boys, to a con man like Rodgers, she was an easy mark. Con men smell vulnerability like an animal smells food, and they go after innocence just as voraciously.

"Rodgers kept telling her that they were going to go out," said Diane Robinson. "He kept the pressure up." Unwittingly, he was aided by another employee at the store.

"This woman who worked there, she told Jenny that Rodgers had just the prettiest eyes. She said, 'If I was eighteen years old, I'd give him a run for his money.'"

Jenny was feeling pressured to go out with

Rodgers, not only by him, and his obvious attraction to the opposite sex, but perhaps most of all by her own yearnings. Finally, after one month of a "courtship," Jennifer Robinson finally decided to date Jeremiah Rodgers. The morning of their date, Jenny dressed, kissed her mother good-bye and got on the bus that took her to Pace High School.

Jenny had a crush on her math teacher. It also happened that math was her favorite subject. Perhaps the only thing she enjoyed more was the NJROTC. NJROTC is the acronym for Naval Junior Reserve Officers Training Corps. Established by congressional act in 1984, the NJROTC program is conducted at accredited secondary schools throughout the country by retired navy, marine corps and coast guard officers and enlisted personnel.

The NJROTC curriculum emphasizes citizenship and leadership development, the significance of sea power and naval topics, such as the fundamentals of naval operations, seamanship, navigation and meteorology. Classroom instruction is augmented throughout the year by community service activities, drill competition, field meets, flights, visits to naval activities, marksmanship training and other military training. Uniforms, textbooks, training aids, travel allowance and a substantial portion of instructors' salaries are provided by the navy.

"I want to be the first woman to drive a tank in the marines," Jenny told her mom earnestly. "Or maybe open a day-care center."

Jenny loved working with kids and thought if the marines didn't work out the way she wanted, her own day-care center would be a great way to make a living. Diane had raised her children that way— to make their own way in the world and not rely on anyone else.

After school that day, Jenny went over to the Corner Store to stock the shelves. Rodgers came in to talk about their date that night.

"Why don't we leave from here?" Rodgers told Jenny.

It was a smart move. By not picking her up at her home, Rodgers would not have to meet her mother, another witness who could place them together.

"My mom doesn't allow me to leave unless she meets [my friends] and knows who they are," Jenny told him.

Rodgers could see that the girl was holding her ground, and if he wanted her, he would have to agree. They set a time of eight o'clock for him to pick her up at her house. Then they would go out on their date.

It was late afternoon when Jenny came home from work. The sun was still high in the sky. One thing Floridians have over their northern brethren, they are closer to the equator, which means the sun sets an hour later every day. For Jenny, it was extra time to spend with friends. Some of her girlfriends came over and they went out together to Wal-Mart.

Driving up Route 90, Jenny got stuck behind a slow-moving vehicle. Her friends kept coaxing her to pass it, until the car pulled slowly off to the side of the road and stopped in a weed-strewn patch of roadway. Jenny drove past; then her conscience kicked in and she stepped on the brakes. Backing up, she pulled in right behind the car and got out to see if something was wrong. She found an old man behind the wheel.

"Sir, are you all right?" Jenny asked, concerned.

The old man smiled and said that he was fine.

"Just pulled off to let all these cars pass me," he said with a smile, exposing a mouth of broken teeth. "I'm okay, thanks, young lady."

Jenny smiled and ran back to her car.

"Come on, Jenny, let's go," her friends coaxed.

Putting the car into gear, Jenny began to talk about Senior Skip Day, which was tomorrow. It was when seniors got to legally cut school and go to the beach. Jenny was really looking forward to it. She finally got home at 4:30 P.M. and decided to go next door to her big brother Jason's house to hang out for a while.

Jenny worshiped her brother, Jason, older by three years. When she was a child, she would follow him everyplace. "Mom," Jason would complain to his mother, "will you make her come inside. Me and my friends are trying to play." But Jason adored his baby sister and would do anything for her. As they grew, their relationship deepened into friendship and respect. They regularly shared confidences.

Before her daughter went next door to Jason's, Diane Robinson told her that Rodgers had called. "He said he'd call back to speak to you, Jenny," but he hadn't. What she didn't tell her was that another name besides Rodgers came up on the caller ID. That in itself was not odd and that's why she said nothing: many people make calls from other people's homes. What Diane Robinson would not know until later was that Rodgers had called from Lisa Johnson's mother's house.

As for Rodgers, he was getting a little leery of Diane Robinson. After all, she was forcing him to pick up the girl at her house. That really wasn't part of the plan. He would have to look her right in the eye and lie through his teeth. Robinson was a tough character and no pushover for a con man like Rodgers.

Born in Plant City, Florida—the self-described "strawberry capital of the world"—Diane Robinson moved with her parents to Georgia when she was a year old. After only four years there, the family moved to Pensacola, where they planted their roots.

Diane Robinson had led a full life and was still very young, only forty-three years old. Her first son had died at four months from SIDS. Undeterred, she had two more children, Jason, her twenty-year-old, who lived next door, and eighteen-year-old Jennifer. She had been divorced for over seventeen years and was what the media likes to call a "single mom." Diane Robinson supported the family as an administrator with the Central Pacific Insurance Company in Pensacola.

"Jenny's father, Sam, and I split up when Jenny was eight months old," she related. "I divorced him because he never supported his kids. He also had a history of problems with the law. Jenny and Jason didn't have any contact with him until Jason was fifteen and Jenny was thirteen, in 1993."

Sam Robinson contacted Diane's parents. He wanted to see how his kids were doing. "My parents called me and told me what he wanted, so we set something up. I asked Jenny and Jason if they wanted to see him and they said yes."

The family got into Diane's Honda and drove across to Nine Mile Road in Pensacola, where Sam Robinson was living in a mobile home. Diane didn't say much to him. There had been acrimony during the divorce, as there frequently is, and "we had a lot of anger toward each other," Diane said.

Afterward, while driving back, Jenny was quiet for a time and then told her mother, "Momma, I don't like that man."

"You don't have to see him," Diane Robinson firmly replied.

Diane Robinson remembered that conversation while Jenny was upstairs, showering for her date with Jeremiah Rodgers. Diane busied herself in the kitchen. Her company, Central Pacific, was having a fish fry the next day; Diane was making her home-made baked beans for the event.

But cooking baked beans did not prevent Diane from helping her daughter, Jenny, get ready for her date.

"Jenny put on blue nail polish, two different shades of blue mixed together. She was wearing a pair of white jeans, a black-and-white-striped body-suit and a blue denim shirt," she later related.

Jenny was all ready to go out when the phone rang. She picked it up. It was Rodgers, calling from his friend Jon Lawrence's house.

"Man, I'm a little confused about how to get to your house," said Rodgers. "How 'bout we meet up at the convenience store? I promise to drive back to your house to meet your mom."

Jenny agreed and drove up to the store. Rodgers, driving his white Chevy Chevette, pulled in at 7:30 P.M.

"Come on," he urged her.

He wanted to leave without seeing her mother first.

"No," Jenny said firmly.

Diane Robinson was looking out the front window of the house when they pulled up. She noticed that one of the headlamps on Rodgers's white Chevy Chevette, crystal clear in the light of the full moon, was dimmed. The bulb was running down.

"Mom, I want you to meet Jeremiah," said Jenny as she walked in.

For a moment, Rodgers just looked at Diane Robinson. Then he turned on the charm and the smile.

"He looked at me smiling and said, 'Nice to meet you.' He was very pleasant."

For his date with Jenny, Rodgers was wearing a baseball cap, a button-down long-sleeved brown shirt, jogging pants and steel-toed black boots. "The shirt was long-sleeved. Even though he was covered up, I could see through the fabric that he had three tattoos showing. He had dark hair and eyes that were very attractive. He seemed normal."

Rodgers shook her hand and looked her right in the eye.

"Now, Jeremiah, I got some rules I got to tell you about. No drinking and driving with Jenny. She's not old enough to drink."

Diane Robinson had never seen Jenny drink alcohol; she had never seen her drunk. Besides, Jennifer was three years shy of Florida's drinking age of twenty-one. Like most states, it suffered from too many underage drinkers who decided to drink and drive and get into accidents.

"You're over twenty-one, so you can drink," Diane continued, "but I'd prefer if you didn't."

"I have no problem not drinking," Rodgers answered easily.

"Her curfew is one o'clock. If anything happens, call home."

"I have no problem with that either." Rodgers smiled.

Thus reassured, Diane went back to her baked beans. Jenny ran to her room to get her brush.

"Mom, we're going."

Diane Robinson came in, wiping her hands on her apron.

"Where're you going?" she asked.

"We're going to ride around with a few friends," said Jenny.

"Jenny, don't be late."

"Momma, tomorrow is Senior Skip Day."

"I don't care, you come home on time."

"Okay," Jenny answered, disappointed that her mother wouldn't budge on the curfew.

"Do you need any money?"

Jenny looked at Rodgers.

"I got three dollars if I want to buy a drink," he answered. "We're just gonna see some friends."

"I love you," Diane said to her daughter.

"I love you, Mom."

"You have a dim headlight, Jeremiah," Diane Robinson cautioned. "You better be careful or the cops'll stop you."

"Yes, ma'am, I know. We're just gonna see friends."

Rodgers shook hands with Diane Robinson politely, and then she watched them drive away and went back to her beans.

"She was feeling like a woman for one of the first times in her life," Diane would later say about her daughter.

Back in his trailer, Jon Lawrence was writing out a list:

- ✓ Coolers of ice for her meat
- ✓ Strawberry wine
- ✓ Everclear
- ✓ Resharpen main blade/clean the saw and tomahawk
- ✓ Film for Polaroid cam.
- ✓ Galloon size siplock bags, big ones [*sic*]
- ✓ Wash rags
- ✓ Rope
- ✓ Jug of water
- ✓ Extra round post shovel

The mention of Everclear was of particular interest. At 190 proof, Everclear is 95 percent pure grain alcohol, odorless, tasteless and very potent. Among its other uses, it's utilized by cooks, employed for medicinal purposes and added as an ingredient in other alcoholic beverages. But on every bottle is written this caution: "Because Grain Alcohol is clear, tasteless and very potent, it could be very dangerous. Use it carefully for legitimate purposes only."

Lawrence got all the stuff ready, including the Everclear, and put it in his truck. He began chugging back some Bacardi rum, waiting for his partner to show up. "Jeremiah wanted to go pick up his girlfriend first and show her off. He wanted to bring her by the house and let me and Ricky meet her," remembered Jon Lawrence. "Jeremiah didn't really brag about her, but he said she was 'all right.'"

Rodgers finally arrived with his "all right" date. Lawrence looked at her, the diagram from *The Incredible Machine* fresh in the synapses of his brain. The three of them hopped into Lawrence's Ford Ranger for a night out in the dark recesses of the county. It would turn out to be the most successful night in the lives of the "flesh collectors."

CHAPTER 5

May 8, 1998, morning

Jon Lawrence got home about dawn. He tried to relax by watching a video. He had quite a collection.

There was *The Silence of the Lambs,* about two serial killers who were exceptionally bright, Hannibal Lecter and "Buffalo Bill"; *The Donner Party;* and *Hooter Mania, Volume 1.*

The film Lawrence decided to watch was *The Donner Party,* a documentary by Ric Burns that had aired on PBS in 1992 and was later transferred to video. The film chronicled the awful winter of 1846 to 1847, when a group of pioneers stranded in the snows of California's Sierra Nevada Mountains cannibalized each other to survive.

As Lawrence watched the video, Dennis Randall, Diane Robinson's boyfriend, was just getting up at the Robinson home. He had gotten home late from work Thursday night, after Jenny had gone. When he got up on Friday morning, he happened to look in Jenny's room. At that early hour, she was usually getting ready for school. But not that morn-

ing; she wasn't there. Diane was just getting up
when he came back into the bedroom.

"Where's Jenny?" Randall asked.

"Well, ain't she in her room?" Diane replied.

"No, she's not."

Diane quickly got out of bed and looked in
Jenny's room. The bedclothes were intact. It was
clear that Jenny had not come home last night.
Diane Robinson felt that emptiness in the pit of her
stomach that every parent dreads. She tried to
make herself believe that Jenny had just slept with
Jeremiah. She was over at his place and too
ashamed to call. Still . . .

"This ain't like Jenny," said Diane portentously,
"not to come home or call or anything."

For now, there was nothing to be done. Randall
would be there all day before going to work. Diane
had to attend the cookout. Figuring activity would
get her mind off her worries, Diane left with her
baked beans and drove into Pensacola, passing the
Corner Store on the way.

Elijah Waldrop had stopped in there to buy a
pack of cigarettes. Behind the counter was the
woman who had told Jenny that if she were
younger, she would go out with Jeremiah.

"You seen Jennifer?" the clerk asked anxiously.
"She never come home last night and her family's
worried sick."

Elijah said he hadn't.

"You seen your brother?"

"No, he comes and goes everywhere. What did
he do now?"

"Oh, nothing, we just don't know where Jennifer's at. And she had a date with Jeremiah last night"

Elijah didn't let on, but he was worried. While he knew nothing, his intuition was eating at him. "You never know about Jeremiah, he'll do anything," Elijah said later in a statement to police.

He tooled over to Jeremiah's house. No one was home, so he hung out. After a while, he remembered he had to get some gas and other stuff. "So I started to leave. I pulled out of my brother's yard, to go up one street from mine. I turned and there was Jeremiah, hauling ass up the street. He went up Fowler and he whipped over toward Jenny's yard. I thought I saw him stopping, so I kept going," Elijah continued in his statement. Elijah kept driving to his house and "as soon as I pulled up in my front yard, he come, you know, skidding in my front yard."

Jeremiah Rodgers jumped out, brandishing a twelve-pack of Busch beer.

"Man, drink a beer with me," said Rodgers, agitated. "I'm so nervous. I'm gonna go to prison! I'm gonna die for this!"

"Slow down, tell me what in the hell you did."

"Well, man, you gotta, you gotta swear to me, swear to me, that you won't never tell nobody."

"If it's something bad, man, I can't swear on it, 'cause you just can't do that. I mean, if it's something bad, man?" his brother asked desperately. "I can't swear on it. You just can't do that."

It was a beautiful day in early spring, when the Panhandle starts to bloom. There was a cedar tree that overhangs the truck for shade. The brothers were standing under it. Elijah sipped his beer. It might have been just another spring day, were it not for the stack of pictures that Rodgers suddenly threw down on the hood of the truck. The stack was almost an inch thick.

"Go on, look," Rodgers urged.

Elijah picked up the pictures, he told police. By his own rough count, Elijah figured there were eight to ten Polaroids in the stack. There were different ones of a girl, positioned in different ways. Elijah didn't see her until he got about halfway through the stack. Then he saw the picture with her face clearly evident. Right then and there, he knew that it was Jennifer.

"What in the hell happened?" Elijah asked his brother.

"That fucking Jon, he shot her! He killed her! Blew her brains out!"

Elijah looked down at the pictures in his hand. There was Jennifer, lying on the ground, with blood all over her face, eyes half lidded and lifeless; Jennifer, with her skin peeled back from her forehead; Jennifer, a knife stuck in her crotch; Jennifer, her knees pulled back to her shoulders, with "everything she had on the bottom" showing; Jennifer, with her right leg from below the knee to the ankle horribly mutilated.

Rodgers claimed that Lawrence seduced, raped, shot and cut her. He pulled the pictures out of Waldrop's hands and brushed them up against his

Levi's shirt to clean them. Then he stuck them for safekeeping in his back right pants pocket.

"What about Justin?" Elijah wondered out loud, beginning to put two and two together. "That sick-ass pervert [Jon], he probably went and killed Justin too, ain't he?"

"Justin was stabbed." Rodgers paused. "I stabbed him first," he admitted to his brother. "Then Jon took the knife from me and stabbed him a lot of times.

"Come on into the woods with me," Rodgers insisted to Elijah. "Come on, and I'll show you the bodies."

He kept coaxing, offering to show him his murderous handiwork. Elijah had the feeling that if he went into the woods with his brother, he wasn't coming back out alive.

"Let's go talk to my brother Lamar," Elijah suggested. "Me and Lamar been through a lot together."

Lamar was Elijah's older brother with the family that had adopted him. Just then, the phone rang. Rodgers picked up the receiver.

"Where's Jenny?" Diane Robinson shouted.

"I don't know who or what you're talkin' about," Rodgers answered casually.

Rodgers liked to watch a lot of movies. In the film *Gaslight*, Charles Boyer tries to make Ingrid Bergman think she is insane when she is not. Jeremiah Rodgers was trying that same tactic—he was going to try and make Diane Robinson believe that they had never met.

"You know very well we have met, Jeremiah!

Don't give me that," Diane continued, showing that she had a helluva lot more sense than Ingrid Bergman.

"'Lady, I'm not fucking responsible for your daughter.'"

That was the moment. There was something in his voice that made Diane Robinson's fears rise sharply and her intuition clicked in.

"Oh, my God! You are responsible."

Rodgers knew he couldn't stonewall her now. She was serious. She'd call in the cops at any second unless he gave her a plausible story he could stick to. Thinking fast, Rodgers stated that during their date, "Jenny got drunk ugly. I had to make her get out, over on Ridge Street."

"Where was your friend Jon?" Diane asked.

"Jon was with us. They [two] just took off after that."

Diane Robinson did not fear that her daughter was dead. To do so would be to give up hope. What mother wants to contemplate her child's death? Besides, there was no evidence yet of anything so drastic. Her mind seized on a better alternative— this pair of scum had raped her daughter. They had then abandoned her in a remote part of the county, where she was lying helpless. She dialed Jon Lawrence's phone number.

"Jon, this is Diane Robinson. Is my daughter there?"

"No one's here," Jon replied in his calm, slow voice. "I haven't seen Red anywhere."

Hopping in her car, Diane drove over to Jeremiah's and saw his Chevette parked in his driveway. "Then a friend of mine rode by Jon's house and saw him wiping out his truck with a white sheet."

It was worse than she had thought. Diane figured Jenny had been beaten, raped and dumped. Jon was wiping up her blood and covering up the crime. Crying hysterically, she called Jeremiah again.

"I don't care what you have done. I will protect you. Help me find my daughter, please!"

Again Jeremiah told her he knew nothing of Jenny's whereabouts and hung up the phone.

"We're going over to Lamar's," Elijah said firmly, and with his brother in tow, they drove over in his truck. Lamar lived in Pace too. For her part, Diane Robinson called the Santa Rosa County Sheriff's Office to report her daughter missing.

And after that phone call, alone, she said a silent prayer to God, imploring him to bring her daughter, Jennifer, safely home.

According to police documents, Diane Robinson's boyfriend, Dennis Randall, and his friend Leonard Wicks started driving around the neighborhood, trying to find Jeremiah Rodgers. They tried his home, but he wasn't there. Then Wicks's friend tipped him that they might be at Lamar Waldrop's. Randall and Wicks drove over. Just as they pulled into the driveway, Elijah pulled up in his truck. Rodgers was next to him.

Car doors slammed. Lamar heard them and

came out. Rodgers and Elijah went over to talk with him while Randall and Wicks stood in the driveway and tried to figure out what to do next. Randall and Wicks couldn't hear what was said.

"Lamar," Elijah told his brother, according to his statement, "Jeremiah is wanting me to go ride down the road with him and I want you to go with me."

Lamar didn't understand. They walked into the living room to talk.

"Jeremiah knows all about that girl that's missing. Let him tell you."

Rodgers told Lamar, "Jon Lawrence was the one that killed the girl." Rodgers was anxious to show Lamar the photographs. They walked into the bedroom for more privacy. Rodgers handed over the stack. Lamar grabbed them and didn't even get more than a glance of the top photo before he said, "Oh, I can't, here," and gave them back to Rodgers.

And once again, treating them like the sacred relic they were to him, Rodgers brushed them off on his Levi's shirtfront and shoved them into his back pocket. The trio went back outside. Lamar went up to Wicks; Rodgers and Elijah stayed back.

"The last one seen Jennifer was Jon Lawrence," Lamar told Wicks.

"That isn't going to be good enough," Wicks said firmly. "I can't let Jeremiah leave."

"Come on, Elijah, I'll take you into the woods," Rodgers urged while Lamar kept talking.

"No," Elijah answered just as firmly. "I'm gonna take you to your car and you just do whatever, 'cause I'm calling the law."

"Well, I'm turning myself in," Rodgers snapped back. But he was scared that if and when he did, the cops would beat his brains in.

In later statements to police, Lamar and Wicks related what happened next.

"No, they won't," said Lamar, who had come over and had overheard. "I know some friends where you won't be hurt. Get in your car and go to Lisa's, park and you stay right there. I'll call you over there because I know a cop."

"Which one of you went out with Jennifer Robinson last night?" Wicks interrupted.

"Yeah?" said Jeremiah Rodgers, turning at the question.

"Don't you have a conscience?" Wicks asked Rodgers. "Don't you? Come over to Jenny's house and meet her momma. You didn't bring her home last night. She wants to know where she's at," he pleaded.

"I feel bad, but I don't know where she is," Rodgers said. "She was with Jon Lawrence."

The brothers turned.

"I can't let y'all leave," Wicks shouted. "Y'all got to come talk to Diane, tell her something, you know; you got to tell her something. You have to get in the truck and ride with us."

Rodgers tried to gauge these two guys. There was the distinct possibility that like many in the Panhandle, they had shotguns in their car, maybe even rifles and a handgun. To say no might mean his death, or worse.

The South has a tradition of lynchings. It's not

something Southerners are proud of or even like to talk about, but it's there, lurking in its recent past. People in the area could still remember when blacks were lynched because of their skin color. Whites had been lynched too on occasion, when there was a perception that doing so was the only way to achieve justice.

After a few tense moments, Rodgers said, "I'll get in the truck and ride with you."

Elijah sidled up quietly behind Wicks.

"Don't come up behind me," Wicks said, suddenly aware of his presence. Rodgers was walking toward the truck, not sure whether to get in or stay out.

"The last place I seen her was with Jon Lawrence," Rodgers implored. "Jon Lawrence has guns! He's crazy!"

Slam!

Elijah slammed the back of the truck with his hands. Rodgers and the other two turned at the sound. A second later, Rodgers ran after his brother. Elijah opened the door of the truck, looked inside and shouted, "It ain't in there," shut the truck door and ran toward the house.

Randall and Wicks took the comment to mean there was supposed to have been a gun in the truck. But it hadn't been there. Instead, Elijah had left it in the house and was running to get it. They didn't have any weapon. Elijah might be getting a pump action or something equally as deadly.

"I ain't going to let y'all do this here; I ain't going to let ya'll do this here," Randall shouted.

Then the door burst open again and the brothers made a run for it. Before Wicks and Randall could react, Elijah was at the wheel of his truck with Rodgers beside him. Cranking up the engine, he put her in reverse. Brakes squealing, he drove off. Wicks and Randall hopped in their car and followed. Elijah turned the corner and kept going, picking up speed and distance.

Far up ahead, Wicks saw the vehicle coming around a corner. Still moving, Jeremiah Rodgers executed an expert forward roll out the passenger door that would have made a movie stuntman proud. Rising to his feet, he quickly got into his white Chevette parked in the driveway.

"He just literally disappeared," Wicks later told police. "I don't know where he went."

Elijah Waldrop's memory of his brother's quick exit is more detailed in his police statement.

"I dropped him off at [his] house and he got in that little Chevette, a one-of-a-kind car. It's got two little palm trees beside the word 'Sheriff' on the back window. No tag. No insurance. All he had was a little piece of brown poster board where the tag is supposed to be. He left the house and went up the street toward East Spencer Field Road. He took a left and that was the last I seen of him."

Frustrated that they had failed to stop Rodgers from escaping, Dennis Randall and Leonard Wicks drove over to the Lawrence compound. Jon Lawrence was home, watching TV.

"This guy Rodgers says you were with him and Jennifer yesterday?" asked Wicks.

"I don't know anything about it," Jon Lawrence

answered fervently, head down. "I don't know Jeremiah Rodgers and I don't know this Jenny, but if I can help find her, I will," he promised. "I wish I could help," Lawrence added, feigning sincerity.

Something about Lawrence and the way he spoke made the two men feel sorry for him; it took all the wind out of their sails.

"We left him," Wicks recalled to police. "And that's all he really told us. He didn't tell us anything other than he didn't know her. Period. I mean, he acted, he didn't act scared or nothing, you know, like he was nervous or anything like that. And we . . . actually believed him."

Back in the car, Wicks and Randall scoured the neighborhood.

"We looked all over, back over by his girlfriend Lisa Johnson's house, and I looked in the old trailers behind the school, where when we was kids, we used to go running," said Randall.

Everyone in Pace knew the place. But they weren't there or anyplace else. They even searched up the dirt roads behind the high school, to no avail. After a while, they gave up and went back to Diane Robinson's house to see if anyone had heard anything there.

Out on the road, the community had become active in the hunt. Civilians patrolled Pace's roads—friends and family of Diane Robinson's, up and down the river, down over to the interstate, back toward the Wal-Mart and up in back of the high school, all looking for one thing: Jennifer Robinson, who was hopefully alive.

It just wasn't like Jenny to suddenly disappear. She had to be in trouble; she had to be found. By then, there were twenty-odd people organizing things. Some were in charge of the search; others were handing out flyers with Jenny's picture, name and description all over Pace, Milton and Pensacola.

Back at her house, Diane Robinson's emotions alternated between fear and hope.

"My dad, my brothers, we called all of Jenny's friends, we searched and searched throughout the day," said Diane. "We came up with nothing."

As for Elijah, by the time he got back to brother Lamar's, people were already there wondering what the hell was going on. Did Elijah know something about Jenny Robinson's disappearance?

"Everybody was, like, *what's going on?* Tell us everything that happened. I couldn't tell 'em, I was so shook up," said Elijah.

Jenny's uncle Hoyt was there.

"If you know something, you need to tell us," Hoyt said to Elijah.

A conscience is a dangerous thing. It can actually make you do the unthinkable.

It is unthinkable to most people that they would ever do something to hurt a relative. Particularly if that relative is part of your immediate family— brother, sister, father or mother. What nightmare could possibly make you choose between your conscience and your family? For Elijah Waldrop, it was not a theoretical question. It was a real situation.

His brother Jeremiah had confessed to being part of a horrific murder. If he was telling the truth and Jennifer Robinson was dead, it was just a matter of time before the cops figured it out. Waldrop picked up the phone and dialed 911.

"I, Elijah Waldrop, was sitting in my truck in the front yard when my brother Jeremiah Rodgers came up and started to tell me about something," he later began as his official witness statement to Santa Rosa County deputies.

CHAPTER 6

Connecting the dots is the policeman's art. Piecing together not only the how but the why of seemingly different crimes is a true talent. But the opportunity to connect those dots has to be presented. Someone has to make the initial link.

When Hand interviewed Diane Robinson, she had told him about Rodgers and Lawrence's potential involvement in her daughter's disappearance. Now another detective had interviewed Elijah Waldrop, who had given a statement that implicated his brother Jeremiah Rodgers in a murder. Everyone in the Santa Rosa County Detective Bureau knew of the Justin Livingston case and that Todd Hand was handling it. They also knew that Rodgers was a suspect in that case. As soon as Rodgers's name came up in regard to Jennifer's disappearance, Hand was notified.

Todd Hand was forced to wonder why Rodgers and Lawrence were now suspects in not one but two murders. How were they linked? As much as Hand wanted to believe Justin Livingston was alive, he really didn't think he was. He figured his body had been dumped or buried someplace where it would be impossible to find, unless you knew where to look.

Rodgers and Lawrence were among the last to see both Justin Livingston and Jennifer Robinson alive. Early investigation showed Rodgers had a date with Jennifer and then left her, supposedly with Jon Lawrence, who was "crazy and has guns." That, plus Lawrence's failure at the voice stress analysis test, meant he knew a lot more than he was telling.

It was late afternoon when Todd Hand drove back out to the Lawrence compound. He found Lawrence at home, watching *Hooter Mania: Volume 1.*

Have you seen Rodgers?" Hand asked.

"No," said Lawrence, head down, his manner as soft and emotionless as ever.

"You know anything about a missing girl, Jon?"

"I don't know anything about that."

"Good. I'm real glad you said that." Hand paused as if he were thinking. "Tell you what," he said at last, "why don't you ride with me to see Elijah Waldrop?"

"Sure," said Lawrence, who rode voluntarily with Hand to see Elijah.

As they drove, Jon Lawrence was calm. His demeanor changed when they turned onto Elijah's street. Suddenly Lawrence got very nervous. Hand didn't want to push him, not yet anyway. Todd Hand turned around and drove back to the Lawrence compound. When they got there, Hand looked out at the house. It was a wretched piece of property.

And he remembered what Elijah Waldrop had said in his statement about a stack of Polaroids.

"Do you have possession of a Polaroid camera or any Polaroid photographs?" Hand asked Lawrence.

"I don't have those things," Lawrence answered.

"I'd like permission to search your cars and your house, okay?"

Hand was treading on shaky constitutional ground. Since he didn't have a search warrant in his possession, he couldn't legally search anything. The only way to conduct such a search was for Lawrence to give consent.

Most criminals think that an innocent man would offer such consent. Instead, the innocent man is more likely to say no precisely because he knows his constitutional rights. Being a criminal, Jon Lawrence said yes to Hand's request. He signed consent forms allowing Hand to go prowling through his home.

Once inside, Hand found Polaroids that had been cut into pieces and deposited in the garbage container. A quick rearrangement of the pieces into some sort of semblance of order revealed what looked like a young woman's body. The face looked like Jennifer Robinson's. Hand went outside, looking up at the sun, still bright and warm on the spring day.

Todd Hand now knew that Jon Lawrence was lying. The presence of the Polaroids in his house proved that. Why else would Lawrence have them if he wasn't in some way involved? He could conduct a more thorough search, but he still had no warrant; Lawrence's consent to search could only go so far. The first priority was reading him his constitutional rights. If Lawrence was subsequently charged with a crime, the situation needed to be constitutionally clean.

Casually Hand reached into his jacket pocket and took out the Miranda card that every cop in Santa Rosa County carried. He did not announce that Lawrence was under arrest; Jon Lawrence wasn't, not until Hand read him his rights and made sure he understood them.

"Jon, would you mind answering some more questions?"

"I don't mind."

"Jon, you have the right to remain silent. Do you understand?"

"Yes," Lawrence answered.

"Anything you say can and will be used against you in a court of law. Do you understand?"

"Yes."

"You have the right to the presence of an attorney. Do you understand?"

"Yes."

"If you cannot afford one, one will be appointed for you by the court. Do you understand?"

"Yes."

"Jon, do you own a Polaroid camera?"

"No."

"Do you have any Polaroid photographs in your possession?"

"No."

"You know what a Polaroid camera and photographs are?"

"Sure," said Lawrence, perplexed.

"Jonathan Lawrence, you're under arrest for the murder of Jennifer Robinson."

Vilma Barnes had no reason to think it was anything but a typical morning. A maid at the Gregson Motel, off Interstate 10, she got to work at about 6:20 A.M. Within five minutes, more or less, it was the time she got to work every day.

She went to the office to pick up the room keys and talk with the desk clerks for a few minutes. Then she walked around and headed to the laundry room to get her supplies and get started. Vilma unlocked the laundry room door, went in and took the cleaning rags out of the washer and put them in the dryer. Vilma turned when she heard the door slam shut a second time. She thought it must be the maintenance man. Instead, facing her was a man who pointed a gun at her head. He held his other hand, palm up.

"Listen, I'm not going to hurt you," said Jeremiah Rodgers. He looked a bit disheveled, like he'd slept in his clothes, which he had. "I just want your car. I need your car. I'm not going to hurt you. Give me your keys."

The safety was off. The gun was loaded. The hammer was back, ready to fire. Vilma began to panic. The last thing Rodgers needed was to shoot somebody out in the open where people could see. He lowered the gun.

"I'm not going to hurt you," Rodgers repeated.

"Okay," Vilma replied.

"Walk with me to your car," he said, taking her gently by the elbow. "Don't try anything; all I want is your car. [When I'm done,] you'll find it three miles down the road."

"Okay."

Vilma walked out of the laundry room first.

"Don't be my second victim today," Rodgers warned.

Halfway to the lot, she held up her keys, making it easy for him to get away and out of her life. Rodgers grabbed them.

"All right," he said, "you can walk back to the laundry room when I'm gone."

"Can I stand here and watch you leave in my car?" Vilma asked.

"No, just go back to the laundry room until I'm gone."

"Okay."

Quickly Jeremiah got behind the wheel of Vilma Barnes's blue Chevy Corsica and shifted the automatic transmission into drive. He headed out of the lot and onto Interstate 10 east. He wasn't sure what he was going to do when he got to Lake County. At least he would be home. But he had given his word to that girl back there and he intended to keep it.

* * *

The day before when he had tumbled out of his brother's car and gotten behind the wheel of his '84 Chevy Chevette and driven out of Pace with the cops—he felt certain—on his heels, a hazy plan had formed in his mind to drive south, back to his home county. Just get on Interstate 10 eastbound, then go south to Lake County and visit his sister. Yes, that was it. Then he'd be on home ground. He could figure out his escape from there. But it just wasn't Jeremiah Rodgers's day, it seemed, when his Chevette broke down soon after getting on Interstate 10.

He had pulled onto the shoulder and parked. He looked around at the soaring palm trees and bushes lining the roadway and smelled the moist air coming in off the Gulf. Cars whizzed by. No one stopped to offer assistance. Rodgers walked to the last exit. As he trotted down the off ramp, he tried not to attract attention—though a pedestrian on a Florida highway is an unusual occurrence.

Rodgers had gone to the nearest motel off the highway that he could find. The sign said GREGSON MOTEL. He went toward the back and stayed there for several hours while walking all over the place. He went to a couple of convenience stores and two adjacent motels.

"I was trying to find a car that would get me all the way down to Lake County," Rodgers later explained. "I didn't want to rob anybody or hurt anybody to get the car, so that night I ended up sleeping in an abandoned car," adjacent to the Gregson Motel.

Rodgers's mind had raced that night. He had the

same recurrent nightmare: Justin's open eyes in the grave when the blanket had come off his face. He awoke in a sweat about four o'clock the next morning. He walked around the motel a little bit more and sat on the steps out back until it got light.

"People started leaving, packing their stuff and leaving."

Could Rodgers fire his gun if he had to—without Jon Lawrence backing him up? A thirty-year-old white woman, with shoulder-length blond hair, wearing an apron like she was a maid, walked by where Rodgers was standing.

"Hi," he had said. "Hi, how are you doing?"

Vilma Barnes had made no reply. He watched her go into the laundry room. She left the door open and he walked in behind her. That's when Vilma Barnes and Jeremiah Rodgers met briefly.

He spared her life and stole her car, the one he promised to give back. But he never did; he had lied, as usual.

The rest of the trip to Lake County was a bit blurred. He would later remember stopping for gas off one of the exits, paying with money from his pocket, money that soon ran out. When it did, he stole. Rodgers wasn't sure if he just filled it up at some stations and then drove off before the attendant had a chance to stop him, or just stole some money someplace and paid in cash. Whatever. Didn't matter.

It was a new day, but one that promised to be quite long. Jeremiah Rodgers was very, very tired.

May 9, 5:45 P.M.

Back in Pace, Jon Lawrence had been taken into custody and was down at the Santa Rosa County Sheriff's Office being booked. At 5:45 P.M., Todd Hand served a search warrant on Lawrence that allowed them to search his place. Quickly the cops drove back to Pace.

When they got to the house, Hand opened the trunk of his car and they each took out a pair of plastic gloves from a box and put them on. They were met at the scene by crime scene technicians (CSTs) of the Florida Department of Law Enforcement (FDLE) and sheriff's office personnel to begin their grim task. Inside, Hand stood for a moment, looking around, taking it in and getting the feel for the place. It was a mess, just like Jon Lawrence's life. Even knowing that Jon lived on a limited disability income, Hand still couldn't help but be repelled by the obvious sense of chaos and decay all around him.

Hand looked at some handwritten notes that he found in a pile of papers on a desk. He read them over, mulling the significance of a list. That unusual manifest was just the beginning of his discoveries. There were weapons of all kinds. Kung fu–style throwing stars were mixed in with a black powder derringer; there were pairs of Smith & Wesson handcuffs and nunchucks, plus a lot of live ammunition. There were KKK booklets, wigs, knives, bomb material, survivalist items, skin books and a bunch of other stuff. And then there was the blood spatter. It was still on the ceiling above the table.

The day before when Hand had spoken to Jon's mother, she had told him how her other son had died from an accidental shotgun blast. The incident, which happened at a party, had affected Jon quite a bit. Ironically, one of the guests at the party was the same person who sold the .380 pistol to Jon. As the cops roamed methodically around the house, they found themselves looking at the blood spatter on the ceiling above the kitchen table that had never been cleaned up.

Farther into the house, things got cramped within rooms that seemed to be overflowing with detritus. Hand and McCurdy kept searching for evidence to tie Lawrence into the disappearances and possible murders. The old house was just packed with stuff. They found themselves in a room where the windows had heavy curtains and the floors were packed with boxes and trunks. Hand was back in one of the corners of the room on his hands and knees, crawling around with his flashlight, between all the junk and the spiderwebs.

"As my flashlight moved about one foot in front of my face," Hand remembered, "I met a possum, who growled and showed his many teeth. I've played sports all my life, but I never moved so quickly and with minimal movement. I found myself on McCurdy's back, trying to get out of the room ASAP. I scared the shit out of him also. After about thirty seconds, we laughed our asses off."

Hand made a list of the things the Santa Rosa cops found and confiscated during their search:

1. Coping saw
2. Black throwing knife with nylon sash
3. Hunting knife with electrical tape on handle
4. Box for Lorcin .380 pistol
5. Winn Dixie receipt showing purchase of Polaroid film
6. 1 cut Polaroid photograph
7. 1 nylon tent
8. 1 tent cover
9. 1 pair used latex gloves
10. Four handwritten notes
12. 1 Pepsi twelve pack container containing cut up Polaroid photograph

The photographs were some of the shots Jeremiah had taken of Jennifer after she had died. In one Polaroid, someone seemed to have cut out part of her head.

The FDLE CSTs were looking for material they could use for DNA matching. They wanted to be able to tie Lawrence to Jennifer Robinson. Their list was longer and included empty beer bottles, the contents of the bathroom's trash can, loose hair, a glass goblet, an empty Doral cigarettes package and three Pepsi cans. They also found a pair of bolt cutters.

Among the porn videotapes they found in

Jonathan Lawrence's possession were *Forbidden Obsessions* and *Nasty Wild Bunch*. Jon had magazines and books that police classified as "devil worshiping literature, among which was an application to become a member of the Church of Satan." At its Web site, http://www.churchofsatan.com, the Church of Satan gives a history of its beliefs:

". . . we are . . . openly dedicated to the acceptance of Man's true nature—that of a carnal beast, living in a cosmos which is permeated and motivated by the Dark Force which we call Satan."

It was a philosophy that appealed to Jon Lawrence. But he probably would have had trouble following through on it, just like every other thing in his life, especially if there were any black Satanists. Jon hated blacks.

While the Church of Satan did not solicit memberships, one could join for a onetime registration fee of $100, which included an embossed membership card.

No such card was found among Jon Lawrence's possessions. Apparently, he hadn't sent the hundred bucks. But there were all kinds of notebooks filled with Jon's ramblings on everything from the weather to family matters. In one particularly chilling notebook section, Lawrence described his thoughts of what appeared to be the perfect date. Jon fantasized about having a relationship with a woman, and that he, Jon, had set the table for a quiet dinner for two.

"When she gets to the house," Jon wrote in notes that police confiscated as evidence, "I take her in the room and fuck her. Then I would slice her stomach open, clear all of her guts out so there's nothing but a shell then take the dead body and re-cline fucking in a half sitting position at the dinner table. I then fill her open stomach full with ice."

Lawrence's preferred method of death, slicing the victim's stomach open and filling it with objects, was actually a preferred way of killing a person and making them disappear during the past century in the Panhandle. In the early 1800s, murderers prowling the canebrake would rob their victims, then kill them with gun, knife or by battering with a stone. To obliterate the evidence of the crime, they would gut the victim, fill his innards with rocks, then drop him in a nearby lake or river. The rocks would cause the body to fall to the bottom, where it would never be seen again.

As the nineteenth century wore on, into the twentieth century, this method of killing fell by the wayside in favor of more sophisticated means. Lawrence, though, had heard stories about it, and those stories must have stuck in his mind. In his fantasy, anyway, he preferred the nineteenth-century way of disposing of a body. But it was also a particularly painful and horrific way to die, which exemplified the violent side of his personality.

Why Lawrence would prefer ice in the body cavity instead of rocks was anyone's guess. He may have thought in some way that the ice would preserve the body while, at the same time, allowing him to weigh it down. However, Hand knew from experience that to ascribe rational thoughts to a functioning schizophrenic with homicidal tendencies could be an exercise in futility. Usually, this kind of individual wasn't aware himself of what made him tick. Even the most expert criminologists were stymied when it came to understanding fully a sociopath's murder fantasies.

In another entry, Jon wrote of a real trip he took to the Smoky Mountains, during which a friend "cussed some niggers," an activity Jon apparently found amusing. Railing against his fate, Jon wrote: "Hail, hail, when the lights out! We're all dead now and courageous. Now I'll say then you're all crazy and I'll say now. God's a fake out. Yeah!!"

Outside, Lawrence's truck was impounded as evidence. The CSTs took a swab of blood from the tailgate liner. If it matched the victim's, it meant she was killed close by.

From the kitchen, the techies removed a blue-and-white Rubbermaid ice chest filled with melting ice and cold water. Nothing else was inside it. One cop noticed a device on the coffee table that he took at first to be a bong, a water-cooling device used to smoke marijuana. It was later identified as a penis pump. Penis pumps attempt, by creating a suction, to enlarge the penis. Some manufacturers claim the process works permanently with the frequent user seeing a size increase.

Further searching led the CSTs to the freezer. They took a plastic bag from it and studied its contents. Inside was some sort of meat and gristle. They weren't sure what it was, so it was impounded as evidence. When checked in at the property office in the rear of the sprawling sheriff's complex, it was refrigerated to maintain its integrity as evidence.

Back at headquarters, Hand showed Lawrence his handwritten list, the one they had found in the pile of papers on Lawrence's desk. Jon looked at it.

"What happened, Jon?" Hand asked gently.

"Jeremiah took the girl out on a date and brought her to my house. Then we all three drove up to Blue Springs. We were gonna wait for my girlfriend up there. As we waited, we drank. Then Jeremiah had sex with her in the cab of my truck. After that, Jennifer was walking in front of Jeremiah. Jeremiah pulled the gun and shot her in the head with a .380 pistol."

Jon had blurted it all out, apparently in a moment meant to ease his conscience. Or maybe he was just trying to find an edge, putting all the blame on his buddy.

"What happened then?"

"She fell, to the ground. I was surprised that Jeremiah had done it."

"Where's the body now?"

"We buried her where she was shot."

"And the photos?"

"Jeremiah took some Polaroids of Jennifer after she died."

The Lawrence house was sealed with crime scene tape. That way, if the CSTs needed to go back in, the home would be in "pristine" condition. This would also prevent anyone else from going in.

As for Jon Lawrence, it really made no difference what he said—without bodies. Without the body of Jennifer Robinson and without the body of Justin Livingston, it would be terribly difficult to make a case, let alone a conviction. Only in very rare cases can cops make a case against a suspect without a body. And only in very rare cases will a jury convict without one.

Bottom line, they needed to find Jennifer. They needed to find Justin. They also needed to find Rodgers. The last Hand had heard, Rodgers had stolen a car and was on his way to Lake County. But what he needed most was to understand why. If Justin and Jennifer were missing and presumed dead, what was the motive?

Hand knew that the answer had to be somewhere in Lawrence's and Rodgers's past. It always was. He remembered that Lawrence's uncle had killed a man in 1994 and was on death row for the crime.

PART TWO

PART TWO

CHAPTER 7

The biggest thing to happen to Florida in 1947 was that gender segregation officially ended at the University of Florida.

With World War II over, more women had become interested in attending the University of Florida (UF). The GI Bill, which also applied to women who served during the war, encouraged these female vets to seek higher education. Women married to veterans attending UF also wanted to attend school. So, in 1947, UF finally became a coeducational institution.

That same year, a girl named Iona Carter was born in the Florida Panhandle to a hardscrabble existence. Moving around, she wound up a teenager and an unwed mother in Texas, where she gave birth to a daughter, Laurie. In 1971, twenty-four-year-old Iona and her child, Laurie, moved back to Florida, where she met Elbert Lawrence. Elbert had charm enough to attract Iona. They fell in love and married. Unknowingly, Iona had married an abusive spouse.

According to court documents, Elbert "physically and verbally abused [his wife] Iona frequently. She couldn't go to the grocery store without getting a black eye. He would lay in her bed with guns in her back loaded, with the trigger pulled back."

The psychological damage must have been unimaginable. What had started out as the union of two people would become, in the next generation, society's problem. Iona and Elbert's progeny would be eventually condemned by society as a necrophiliac murderer. Adding to Iona's worries were her husband's extracurricular activities. Court documents linked him to the Ku Klux Klan.

Iona gave birth to a boy who died at seven weeks from a heart condition. Then, when Iona was in her eighth or ninth month of pregnancy with her second child, her parents were in a fatal car accident. Her mother died instantly while her father lingered. Every day that her father was in the hospital, Iona was there, on her feet, despite her condition. With no chance of recovery, he mercifully died.

Iona gave birth on April 12, 1975, to a boy they named Huey Alec Lawrence. (When Huey grew older, he would be renamed Jonathan.) During his first year of life, baby Huey suffered from frequent fevers and had to be dunked in a tub of ice to break them. Huey writhed in pain and screamed at the top of his lungs. Iona could not stand her baby's screaming.

Despite the fevers of his infancy, Huey Lawrence was a good-looking child with sparkling eyes. He liked to laugh, to run, to play with his siblings, like any other kid. He still had his humanity. He wasn't cruel and he didn't hurt. So what changed him?

Criminologists constantly speculate about killers' personalities and motives. Frequently they don't go back far enough to find the root cause. In Jon Lawrence's case, the real turning point in his life was when he was four years old, in the car with his parents, on a dark night in the canebrake.

Elbert was driving. He got drunk and forced Iona, dead tired, to drive. She fell asleep at the wheel and smashed into a ditch. Hospitalized for three months, Iona was plagued for years thereafter with severe leg damage. Meanwhile, Huey's head hit the back of the seat as the car went up.

Huey measurably declined after that accident.

"He was just kind of like in a dreamworld," Iona said in court papers. "Kind of dense, slow. Slow to respond, slow to react. I felt like he could not understand."

Huey's sister, Laurie, said he became very shy, slow, withdrawn, nonconfrontational, and kept to himself. Nadine Elizabeth Golson, his aunt, agreed. After the accident, she said, "he became real withdrawn. He didn't play with the other brother [Ricky] or my daughter or with the other sister. And he started wetting the bed."

When she would take her young children to play with Huey, they would climb all over the bed while Huey just stood there with his head down, looking like he had no reaction at all. He just wasn't the same; that hit on the head during the car accident would later be diagnosed as having caused severe brain damage.

Huey started kindergarten in 1980, after the accident, but he was consistently slower than the other children. He was held back in the first grade. Some of the children made fun of him. On one occasion, children shot rocks at him with slingshots, and Iona discovered him sitting down in a ditch, crying.

Kids can be cruel. They sometimes have trouble curbing their primitive tendencies. The kids in Huey's school were very cruel toward a vulnerable, already messed-up kid. By second grade, the ones that have not learned to be civilized are especially cruel.

When Huey was in the second grade, kids began making fun of his name, calling him "Huey Pewey." He would come home and cry about it. Iona didn't know what to do until finally she decided to give Huey what he so dearly wanted—a new name. His mother dubbed him Jonathan, and they kept Huey as his middle name.

In the third grade he was repeatedly paddled by his teacher and his principal because they thought Jonathan was not paying attention, but his problem really was that he had no ability to concentrate. One doctor diagnosed attention deficit disorder and prescribed Ritalin, but Jonathan developed a tic and had to stop taking the medication.

Through it all, mother and son developed a strong bond. He was devoted to her. He would do anything for her. Maybe, in some way, he might be able to get her a new leg to replace her injured one. It was a thought he had on more than one occasion. But there was nothing he could do about it, at least not yet. Jon imagined being able to replace his mother's leg with a more functional one, but he couldn't figure out how to do it.

According to court documents, Elbert continued to be abusive throughout Jonathan's childhood, and not only to Iona. Around 1985, when Jonathan was ten years old, he learned that his father had been sexually abusing his older half sister, Laurie, when she was between the ages of twelve and fifteen. Iona had police come to the house and arrest Elbert. She divorced him while those charges were pending. Elbert was sentenced in 1986 to ten years' imprisonment and served four years.

Jonathan seemed to become more withdrawn after Elbert's arrest, although he had become so quiet and so much of a loner that it was hard to tell. "I think it really hurt him," Laurie said. Iona agreed that he "took it hard. He was more withdrawn after his dad left because Elbert was good to the boys."

To Jon Lawrence, the knowledge that his father had sexually abused his half sister was devastating. It made him angry, frustrated and impotent. He just didn't know what to do. Meanwhile, Iona divorced Elbert. The boys drew together after that. Wesley noticed how frequently Jonathan was humiliated and picked on by his peers for no apparent reason. He tried to ignore it, but on one occasion Wesley, who was much like his father, came to Jonathan's rescue and "popped" the bully. This happened on the school bus. The driver got so angry at Wesley because he threw the first punch that he ejected him and told him he couldn't ride on the school bus anymore.

"Mom, I can't stand it anymore because kids are

picking on Jon for no reason," Wesley told Iona. "And Jon, he won't fight back."

Wesley liked to go on hunting and fishing trips. He was a real outdoorsman. Jon, though, never wanted to go. On the rare occasions when he did, Jon couldn't bear to kill or clean the catch.

Around 1987 or 1988, Iona became involved with Ed Thronebery. Iona became pregnant and gave birth to a daughter, Kimberly, when Jonathan was about twelve. But Thronebery was a disaster. He was insanely jealous. On one occasion, Thronebery's son—in front of Jonathan—told Iona that she was too good for his father and his father went off with another woman. That led to a confrontation in which Throneberry shoved Iona, breaking both bones in her already bad right leg.

In 1989, Iona's septic-tank business, which she had been using to support her family, failed. She applied for public assistance, including food stamps and Medicaid. As hard as things were, she provided for the children as best she could. Then, in a final fluke of biblical proportions, their house burned down, destroying everything.

Elbert served his time and he was out on the street again by 1991. According to Elizabeth Livingston, Justin's mother and a Lawrence relative, Elbert kept a shotgun in the house. One night in the trailer in the Lawrence compound, he took it out and began passing it around. A group of teenagers, including Jon and his brother Wesley, passed it around the table.

"Elbert let the teenagers hold it and gave them beer at the same time," Livingston related.

Alcohol and guns never mix and they didn't that night. As the gun was being passed around the table, each man slammed the gun against the floor. It was probably a pump action and by slamming it down, a round went into the chamber without anyone realizing it. The gun got passed to Wesley, who slammed it down on the floor; only this time, it went off.

It killed Wesley instantly, nearly taking off his jaw, and splattering blood all over the place. Jon was devastated. He didn't know what to do with his feelings. He loved his brother and couldn't figure out how such an awful thing could have happened. Jon had all these questions and no answers. Bad things kept happening. It all boiled up in his brain, looking for an outlet.

Like many disturbed kids, Jon Lawrence was vulnerable to "conspiracy nut" philosophies. Whether to the left or right, fascism or communism, it was all fueled by an underlying desire to get out the aggression that had been building up for so many years. Jon Lawrence became a white supremacist.

The racist literature that Hand and McCurdy found in the Lawrence home when they executed their search warrant had its roots back in Jon Lawrence's teens, with his first major crime. Young Jon Lawrence was a troubled teenager who hated blacks. It was not surprising, considering his father's alleged background in the KKK. But Jon Lawrence *really* hated blacks. But he still wasn't a violent guy, not by himself anyway. It just wasn't his style. Jon hung with two guys, Rob Palmer and Brian Terhune, and they saw things in the same skewed way he did.

Alone, he couldn't act, but together, things became possible.

Chumuckla Highway is a small, two-way street. There's nothing notable about it, except the New Macedonia Church, a distinguished-looking wooden edifice. Just before midnight, Jonathan Lawrence drove by the church and parked about thirty feet down on Guernsey Road. Doors slammed as Lawrence and his companions got out of the car.

Brian Terhune and Rob Palmer followed Jon Lawrence up the deserted street to the church. They were carrying a can of gray spray paint. Jon took the can and started spraying the side of the church closest to Guernsey Road. Brian then took the can and sprayed the other side and the church's sign. Rob acted as lookout. His job was to raise the alarm if anyone came along.

They didn't. The streets stayed deserted and the teens did their business. Afterward, they walked away as nonchalantly as they had come. They got in Lawrence's car and drove off into the night as if nothing had happened. Back at the church, the walls shouted out at anyone who chose to look:

ALL NIGGERS MUST DIE

ALL NIGGERS MUST HANG

FUCKIN NIGGERS

KKK

Brian Terhune got nervous. He figured the cops weren't stupid. They'd figure out who was responsible and come after them. He didn't wait; instead, he fingered Jonathan Lawrence. He and Rob Palmer, who also made a deal, filled in the details for the prosecutor John Molchan. A former officer in the United States Navy, Molchan had become a lawyer in the service, serving with the judge advocate general (JAG), and then became a prosecuting attorney when his hitch was up.

"Did you know the church was largely a black congregation?" Molchan asked Palmer.

"Yeah, I did," Palmer answered. "I think Brian and Lawrence knew also."

"Did you warn Brian and Lawrence if someone was coming while they sprayed the church?"

"I would have."

The police theory of the crime was that Palmer was the lookout while the other two did the nasty racist work. Unfortunately for Justin Livingston and Jennifer Robinson, the concept of punishing hate crimes harshly did not exist in 1993 in the state of Florida.

The principle behind tougher sentences for hate crimes is that by deliberately targeting a particular group—religious, racial or otherwise—a perpetrator is hurting all. The same holds true for the use of racial or religious epithets scrawled on religious buildings. By doing so, the vandal is not only hurting the individual congregation, he is hurting anyone who subscribes to that congregation's beliefs.

By 2003, four states still had no hate crime laws:

Arkansas, Indiana, South Carolina and Wyoming. Seventeen states had laws that did not include sexual orientation as a protected group, while twenty-nine, including Florida, had laws that do protect on the basis of sexual orientation. Seven states had hate crime laws covering gender identity. But in 1993, that was all in the future.

In 1993, when Jon Lawrence was eighteen years old, and at the emotional crossroads of his life, hate crime legislation was not common. What would, a decade later, be perceived as a hate crime punishable by a longer sentence would just be perceived as a regular felony punishable by a shorter one. Tried and found guilty on charges of criminal mischief and property damage, Lawrence was sentenced to four years in prison. The Department of Corrections (DOC) Report described him as "an eighteen year old Caucasoid property offender." Ironically, in Florida, race mattered when filling out police forms.

On November 17, 1993, barely a few weeks into his incarceration, Lawrence slashed his wrist in a suicide attempt. The DOC reported that he had a history of attempts to commit suicide with "at least 50 suicidal gestures in the past." Dr. Olga Fernandez diagnosed Lawrence as suffering from "adjustment disorder with depress mood" and "antisocial personality disorder." The *DSM* defines adjustment disorder with depress mood as follows:

". . . the development of clinically significant emotional or behavioral symptoms in response to an identifiable psychosocial stressor or stressors.

The stressor may be a single event or there may be multiple stressors."

In Jon Lawrence's case, there were multiple ones, stemming from his early childhood. The added part of the diagnosis—depress mood—meant that "the predominant manifestations are symptoms such as depressed mood, tearfulness or feelings of hopelessness." That description fit Jon Lawrence to a T. But whereas most depressants only hurt themselves, the Antisocial Personality Disorder diagnosis was an ominous portent of things to come.

Antisocial Personality Disorder is a lifelong pattern of not having a conscience, of not recognizing the boundaries of others, and of manipulating and deceiving others for personal benefit.

The diagnosis—coupled with the facts of Lawrence's scarred background and, so far, brief criminal career—showed that he was a full-blown psychopathic criminal, the most dangerous kind. And though his crimes had yet to involve physical violence, they did involve violence metaphorically. It might only be a matter of time, unless treatment was successful, that Jon Lawrence acted out violently.

After about six months behind bars, the state finally got Lawrence the help he needed when they transferred him to the state mental hospital in Chattahoochee. While the state's intentions were good, fate was about to take a hand in introducing two of Florida's notorious future murderers to each other.

* * *

Jeremiah Rodgers was born on April 19, 1977, and hailed from the town of Altoona in Lake County, Florida.

The county is in the center of the state, in an area called the Central Highlands. While nearly all of Florida is at sea level, Lake County has a relatively high elevation of about 50 to 190 feet above sea level. It's one of the few destinations in Florida with rolling hills to climb.

The place is like a picture postcard, a perfect place for parents to raise kids. The Rodgers family lived there and had two sons and a daughter. They also seemed to have a liking for biblical prophets. The youngest son was named Elijah.

According to the Bible, Elijah lived during the ninth century B.C., in the reign of King Ahab. When Jezebel, Ahab's wife, got the Jewish people to worship the god Baal, Elijah strode into action. He preached that there was only one God of Israel and that the people of Israel were going to suffer a great drought as a result of their polytheism. Turned out, Elijah was right; the drought that followed lasted for three years.

But Ahab and company didn't give up. They wanted a contest of strength to determine the true deity, so 450 prophets of Baal placed a sacrificial bull on an altar. They called on Baal to consume it in fire. Of course, nothing happened. Then it was Elijah's turn.

The prophet Elijah bent over the snorting bull and called on the God of Israel for help. Suddenly a burst of flame instantly consumed the animal.

Taking this as a sign that the God of Abraham was exceedingly unhappy with their transgression, the people rose up and slew the prophets of Baal. God then brought forth rain, ending the drought and the "spell" that Jezebel had whipped up was broken.

The Rodgers family named Jeremiah after the Bible's apocalyptic prophet who, in the end, lost. His own people viewed him as a traitor because he would not support fighting the Babylonians. Instead, he had called for surrender. The kings he worked for rejected this advice. Declared an outlaw, he was placed under guard, from which he watched Jerusalem's destruction by Nebuchadnezzar.

Like their biblical namesakes, the brothers Rodgers had digressive fates. Their parents decided that they couldn't afford to keep both boys. A decision was made to put Elijah up for adoption, while Jeremiah stayed behind. Elijah was adopted by the Waldrop family of Pace and moved north. While Elijah adjusted well, not so Jeremiah Rodgers.

"What I've been told from my dad and my grandma down South was he [Jeremiah] went back and forth between my mom and my dad because he was all the time stealing cars," Elijah Waldrop told police.

Rodgers had an extensive record of grand-theft auto.

"Then, when he was either thirteen or fourteen, he went to a juvenile camp. He moved on from there, on up to jail, and stayed in jail six to seven years," Waldrop later told Assistant State's Attorney Ron Swanson.

In May 1993, Jeremiah Rodgers was arrested and charged with grand-theft auto. He was convicted in August and sentenced to four years and six months of hard time. It was while he was behind bars that prison officials noted certain problems with his personality and transferred him to "the mattress factory" for evaluation. It was a derisive nickname for Chattahoochee that went back to the nineteenth century.

In 1841, Florida officially passed from Spanish to United States control and became a U.S. territory. There were a few primitive county jails in the territory, but nothing like a penitentiary to house convicted felons.

In Chattahoochee, the Florida Panhandle town forty-one miles east of the state capital at Tallahassee, an arsenal had been built prior to 1830. During the Civil War, the place was used to muster Confederate troops who then headed north to fight for slavery and states' rights. After the Civil War in 1868, the U.S. government ceded the arsenal and its grounds to the state of Florida. It was a gracious gesture by a former foe.

Florida turned the arsenal into the state's first penitentiary. Set up on a paramilitary model, its activities were overseen by the Florida adjutant general. About 125 years before Jon Lawrence got there, Chattahoochee beckoned Calvin Williams to her damp, stone corridors in November 1868. Williams, convicted of larceny and sentenced to one year, became Chattahoochee's first prisoner.

He was long gone by 1876, when the state officially closed the prison, transferring the prisoners to other institutions. The buildings at Chattahoochee were then converted into the Florida State Hospital, for "insane" and emotionally disturbed patients. Florida already had a tradition of selling its inmates' services as slave labor to anyone who could pay the price. Seeing a new workforce to be exploited, the patients were made to make mattresses, which were then sold to private industry. That's how Chattahoochee got its nickname, "the mattress factory."

By the time Jeremiah Rodgers and Jonathan Lawrence got there in 1993, Chattahoochee was quite literally a tourist attraction. Though still a hospital that treated the mentally ill, tourists drove through the hospital's grounds. They admired the hospital's administration building. Dubbed "the White House," it was the original officer's headquarters of the arsenal. The original arsenal powder magazine, built between 1832 and 1839, to store arms for the U.S. War Department during the Indian Wars, was in the process of being restored by English artisans.

Rodgers and Lawrence hit it off immediately and became fast friends. Lawrence would listen quietly to Rodgers's boastful comments, while Rodgers put up with Lawrence's moody silences. There was something about their personalities that just meshed, like two becoming one. The doctors found Lawrence in particular to be an interesting patient.

During his time at Chattahoochee, Lawrence was evaluated repeatedly. The diagnosis was the same every time—mentally ill and suicidal. The evaluations began to report that he experienced intermittent command hallucinations—that is, his hallucinations were prompted by the commands of some unseen force. Along with a smorgasbord of previous diagnoses, Lawrence now had a new one: schizotypal personality disorder.

The *DSM* defines schizotypal personality disorder as follows:

"The essential feature of Schizotypal personality Disorder is a pervasive pattern of social and interpersonal deficits marked by acute discomfort with, and reduced capacity for, close relationships as well as by cognitive or perceptual distortions and eccentricities of behavior."

People with this type of disorder "may believe that they have magical control over others . . . are often suspicious [and] paranoid. . . ."

As for Rodgers, he had fantasies of killing one of his doctors, Manolo Sanguillen. They just seemed to have a personality difference. Sometimes Sanguillen would have to put Rodgers in isolation for disobeying rules. Rodgers hated that, naturally. He manifested his feelings in fantasies of peeling off Sanguillen's skin and sewing him back up afterward sans anesthetic. It would be pain, pure pain; that's the way Rodgers wanted it.

But as it turned out, it would be a member of the Lawrence family who killed first.

In 1994, while Rodgers and Lawrence were in Chattahoochee, Jon Lawrence was in the day room, the place where prisoners congregated during the day to play cards or watch TV. Looking up at the TV screen, Lawrence recognized his uncle Gary Lawrence. Uncle Gary was in handcuffs. He was doing the "perp walk." The reporter in Santa Rosa who was covering the story said Gary Lawrence had been arrested for murder.

On the morning of July 29, 1994, a contractor named Charles Haney found a charred body by the side of the road in a new subdivision within Santa Rosa County. Pensacola was expanding into the suburbs, and if Santa Rosa played its cards right, it could be one of those counties that benefited from the burgeoning population's need for affordable housing. Murder, though, is not good for business.

The Santa Rosa County Sheriff's Office worked hard to solve the case. Unknown to them at the time, their quarry was an outlaw named Gary Lawrence. He had been released from prison on January 10, 1994, after serving a three-year term for grand-theft firearm, a holdup with a gun.

After his release, Gary met Angela Bruner and they married. For newlyweds, they had an unusual arrangement—they didn't live together most of the time. In early July 1994, Lawrence finally moved in with his wife.

Angela had gotten friendly with a man, Sam Wheeler. He drove her to work on the hot, humid morning of July 28. He was scheduled to pick her up around noon. When he showed up, he was drunk. They drove to a mutual friend's house, where Wheeler went inside to lie down on the couch and sober up. Soon after, Gary showed up to get his wife.

He noticed Angela went in to check on the guy several times while the others stayed on the porch drinking. Gary later said that he "was tired of see-ing Angela going in to Sam and talking to Sam." He threatened to beat Sam and "sling him through the window." Lawrence and Angela argued about that.

Wheeler finally sobered up. Gary politely con-fronted him with his concerns. Wheeler listened respectfully and they shook hands. Apparently, the jealousy crisis had passed. Together, the three left and arrived back at Angela's apartment at 5:00 P.M.

Just after arriving, Gary Lawrence drew out a bowie knife and threw it on the ground. He wal-loped Sam in the face and body; Sam did not fight back. Angela and her sixteen-year-old daughter, Kimberly, finally separated them. Gary and Sam then walked around the yard and talked it over.

"It seemed like everything was all right," Gary would later remember.

Why Sam would remain in what was an obviously dangerous situation can only be imagined. Two hours later, the three were hanging out again in Angela's apartment like nothing had happened. Sam lay down on the couch while Lawrence and Angela sat together, whispering. The two told Kimberly and a visiting friend, fifteen-year-old Julia Powell, to go into Kimberly's bedroom and stay there. Once the teens had gone, the married couple gathered together several weapons, including a metal pipe and a baseball bat. From the bedroom, where they had taken refuge, the girls heard pounding noises.

"Stop hitting, Gary," they heard Sam say.

What the girls didn't know was that on the other side of the door, Gary had beaten Sam so hard with the pipe that it had bent in half.

"I can't move," the girls heard Sam utter.

Gary Lawrence put the pipe down and picked up the baseball bat. Coldly, he beat Sam with it, until finally Sam didn't move anymore. The court record states that the teens were then called in "and required to assist in the cleanup." They saw that a mop handle had been stuck down Sam's throat.

Satisfied that Sam was dead, Gary and Angela discussed how to get rid of the body. In the end, Lawrence decided to burn it. They went through Sam's pockets and belongings, taking out anything that could ID him. Angela used bleach on the rug and sandpaper on the wood frame of the couch to remove Sam's blood that had spattered there.

It's a common ritual murderers follow, trying to use bleach to cover up their crimes. The problem is, when you kill a person by battering them, their blood flies all over the place. When criminalists examine a crime scene, it is now standard practice to

spray Luminol. It's a chemical that glows under ul-
traviolet light. Just one drop of blood missed and
the Luminol can not only find it, the sample can
then be used for DNA typing.

The couch cushions saturated with Sam's blood
and the weapons were thrown into a pond behind
the apartment. It was, all in all, a pretty good job of
disposing of incriminating evidence. The problem
was, the murder had been spur of the moment, but
too many people knew there was bad blood between Gary Lawrence and Sam Wheeler.

After the Santa Rosa cops identified the burned
body found by the contractor as Sam's, they got
to Gary Lawrence pretty quickly. They interro-
gated Lawrence, who confessed to killing Wheeler.
A jury found him guilty of first-degree murder,
conspiracy to commit murder, theft of less than
$300 and grand-theft auto. At the penalty phase,
on March 17, 1995, Lawrence presented testimony
from his brother, a psychologist and a psychiatrist
who all argued for mercy. The jury was unmoved.
By a vote of a nine-to-three majority, he was sentenced to death.

If Jon Lawrence had been devastated earlier because of his father's incarceration for sexually
abusing his half sister, his psyche took another hit
when his uncle was sentenced to death for murder.
It seemed like there was no hope for the Lawrence
family, no good that was coming from them.
Lawrence could only hope that in some way he
could change the family luck.

While he was in Chattahoochee, and his bond

was formed with Rodgers, he began confiding to his fellow inmate about his family. He told him about his mother, Iona, and his father, Elbert. He told of the Lawrence clan of Pace, which went back generations to Confederate times. And he told of the numerous cousins he had in the area. Rodgers perked up at that one. It made no difference that his friend was confiding in him; whatever knowledge he could get that could give him an edge over somebody, he would use it, even if it meant betraying a confidence or a friend.

Jeremiah Rodgers listened attentively when Jon Lawrence told him of the Livingston family. Maybe there was something there to relate to, the various and similar deprivations that the Rodgers and Livingston families had suffered through. Rodgers got particularly attentive when Lawrence described his cousin Felicia. She was Justin's older sister and a good-looking girl at that. Felicia stayed in Rodgers's mind for quite a long time.

In August 1995, the Florida State penal system let Jonathan Lawrence go. The fact that he was now a functioning schizophrenic made no difference. No legislation existed to keep him behind bars. Nothing in his record indicated a propensity for violence, except of course his background. That left his newfound buddy, Jeremiah Rodgers, all alone in Chattahoochee.

While Jon Lawrence went home to Pace, Jeremiah Rodgers passed another year in the hospital, a psychopath who charmed everyone with his smile and good looks. When he was approaching his release date, he decided to put his charisma to work. He decided to try it on a female first. Jeremiah Rodgers began writing a series of letters to Felicia Livingston.

Jeremiah Rodgers is a good writer—one of his many skills is the ability to turn a phrase, despite an inferior formal education. He knew it too, because his letters to Felicia Livingston were not the only time during this case that he used his writing talents to his advantage.

In his letters to Felicia, he described in sympathetic terms the damage he had caused people and his painful regret. Using the twelve-step jargon prisoners learn from support groups, Rodgers said that he was taking responsibility for his life while knowing that God really controlled it. He explained how he was going to make amends to the people he had hurt.

Rodgers said that when he got out of prison, he wanted to start a whole new life. Maybe settle down someplace and get married and have kids. He was a talented tattoo artist and massage therapist. Maybe he could broker those skills into some good-paying jobs. It was as convincing a con as any Jeremiah Rodgers had ever done, and it worked.

Of course, Felicia was fooled. She wrote him back that she would look forward to seeing him when he came to visit. Rodgers had previously made it clear in one of his letters that after he got out he intended to come out to Pace and stay with his buddy Lawrence for a while until he got situated. Of course, he never told Felicia that, in his mind, getting situated meant finding some woman he could leech off with his good looks, body and smile.

With that connection set up, Jeremiah Rodgers next turned to his family. Who could he use there? It was a coincidence that Elijah Waldrop, his brother, had been adopted by a Pace family and that Jon Lawrence came from the same town. But his philosophy was that life is full of coincidences and you'd be crazy not to make the most of them.

Thus began another series of correspondence. Rodgers probably spent more money on writing supplies than any of the convicts in Chattahoochee. This time, Rodgers began writing a series of letters to Elijah Waldrop, who responded.

"We started writing about a month before he got out," Elijah told police. "I just got a letter from him. I guess he got my mailing address and my phone number from my sister. He [started] calling me three to four times a week."

Phone calls from prisons have to be collect. Because covnersations go all over the country and sometimes internationally, one can't have some con standing there, plunking quarters into the phone, while a line of murderers, armed robbers and rapists wait patiently on line for their turn. These are not a patient kind of people.

What most prisons do to save time and to prevent turbulence is have the cons make their calls collect. The prison administration contracts with a company in the private sector to provide this service, which it does, at enormous rates, sometimes as high as twenty-five cents a minute. But Rodgers didn't care. What did he care how many calls he made, or how long they were? He wasn't paying for it, his brother was.

So they talked. And the con man did what con men do—he gained confidence. It didn't matter to Rodgers that the person he was conning was his brother. He didn't know any other way to be.

"I mean, at that time, I didn't know, I would never think that my brother would do something like this in the future. So I figured I'd give him a chance and he's, like, 'well, stay in touch with me. Let's write and all 'cause I don't know when I'm gonna get out of jail.'"

Rodgers, of course, knew when he was going to get out of jail. He knew that he could persuade the parole board into letting him out.

"So I gave him a chance and I was writing him letters back and I sent him a picture and he never did send me none in return," Waldrop recalled. "All he sent me was letters. He was telling me about how he conned people in jail to get by and buy cigarettes at the canteen. Then he calls me up one Thursday afternoon. He was being released the following Wednesday. I told him I'd be there."

Jeremiah Rodgers's con was complete. He had managed to convince his brother of his good intentions and love. And when Rodgers walked out of Chattahoochee, there was Elijah Waldrop. The two brothers embraced. Elijah figured Rodgers was coming to Pace to be with him. He was wrong, of course. Rodgers had an agenda.

When he got to Pace, Rodgers was going to look up his old friend Lawrence. He was going to look up Felicia Livingston and see what he could get out of her. And he was going to stay with his brother for a while and see what he could get out of him.

Waldrop took three days off from work to be with his brother. He was really looking forward to getting to know Jeremiah for the first time. Elijah took Rodgers with him back to Pace to meet his parents. Rodgers settled in. One night, Rodgers joined Elijah for a trip over to Elijah's cousin Sam Webster's house. The twentysomethings sat around, playing quarters for beer, and then Lisa Johnson came over. She was a friend of Sam's.

Rodgers and Lisa hit it off. They moved in together with a unique arrangement—Rodgers had the freedom to go out and sleep with other women. To say that Lisa had a problem with self-esteem is putting it mildly.

"He stayed at our house on Polk Avenue for probably a month and then he moved in with Lisa," Elijah remembered. "When Lisa would piss him off, he would go stay with Jon, and get drunk, or they'd smoke a joint or, you know, just hang out. I said, 'Well, whatever you do is your business.' We wasn't really getting along [at that point]."

Rodgers drifted south, back to Lake County, where he still had friends. He stayed there for a while until he got bored and then returned to Pace, where he lived part of the time with Elijah, part of the time with Lisa, and hung out with Lawrence, just as they had at Chattahoochee. There was something about the way that they mixed, the way they complemented each other. They each had a degree of craziness that was heightened when they were together, and they each got a kick out of that.

"When Jeremiah first went to visit Jon, Jon gave him a Satanic bible," says Elijah in official records.

"Jeremiah, you better throw that trash out in the yard," Elijah told him.

The Satanic bible was written by Anton Szandor LaVey. His birth name was Howard Stanton Levey, but Anton Szandor LaVey sounded like a better name for a Satanist. LaVey was born in 1930 and led a knockabout existence until the night of April 30, 1966. During the German Satanic festival of Walpurgisnacht, LaVey had an epiphany.

In what would later be described as a "blinding flash," he pronounced himself the High Priest of Satan. Thus, he proclaimed that the Age of Satan had begun, and he founded the Church of Satan as a religious institution. His life's work, the Satanic bible, came out of these modest beginnings. The Satanic bible came out of the Satanism and witch-craft fad of the latter part of the 1960s.

Thinking there was a market for a book on Satanism, paperback publisher Avon Books con-tracted with LaVey to produce such a tome. The book has since become de rigueur reading for Satanists. In it, LaVey argues for a "new religion separate from the 'traditional' Judeo-Christian definitions of Satanism."

Elijah Waldrop was not about to have anything regarding Satan in his house.

"I didn't believe in that. Me and my brother got in a little argument about that, but it's my house, my rules. You live with me, you're gonna go by what my family believes in."

On another occasion, Rodgers told his brother, "Jon's got a friggin' arsenal; he's got knives and he's got plenty of everything."

When he finally did visit, Elijah was startled by the insides of Jon's house. There were skeletons all over, posters of skeletons on motorcycles. Swastikas lounged next to pentagrams on Jon's dresser, next to books about Satanic rituals. Someplace in his mind, Jon thought he could get meaning from hate. Rodgers found Jon's place rather comfortable.

It was in that trailer that Rodgers's fantasies of violence and Lawrence's neuroses took shape in reality. Hour after hour, Rodgers and Lawrence talked about bringing their violent fantasies to life: robbery, rape, mutilation, murder. Rodgers had an idea to construct an underground prison. He told Lawrence that he would "keep people" whom he "did not like" there and do "weird things" to them. Hazy plans to implement their fantasies began to form in their minds.

Plans became reality when they executed a makeshift plot that culminated with their murder of Justin Livingston. Next they talked about killing Jennifer Robinson. They planned it out and then, finally, came the night that Jeremiah Rodgers had his date with her.

CHAPTER 8

Jennifer Robinson was a smart girl, smart enough to be wondering what kind of relationship her date had with Jon Lawrence, the friend he was bringing along. Or maybe she felt having the friend along would make things safer.

Two things are clear. First, Diane Robinson had not raised her daughter to ride off into the country with two criminals. Jeremiah Rodgers was a con man who would normally trick people into liking him with his charm and good looks. That had worked on Jennifer. Otherwise, she wouldn't have been with him.

Second, Jon Lawrence, who had already been diagnosed as a functioning schizophrenic, was able to repress his delusional behavior long enough to appear passive, his usual face to society. Despite that face, or because of it, he had thoughtfully brought along Everclear. It is the most potent liquor available. It is considered so dangerous to consume that many states ban its sale within their borders.

The truck headed up to Blue Springs, deep into the most rural section of Santa Rosa County. They stopped at a convenience store, bought some gas,

Mountain Dew and Dr Pepper, got back in and went straight out to Blue Springs. They drove as far as they could in the four-wheeler into the canebrake, until it was so impenetrable they could go no farther. They stopped and talked for a minute and finally Rodgers got out of the truck; Jennifer stayed inside.

The windows were open and the threesome passed around a spiked Mountain Dew. Jon didn't take very much. Apparently, having had the rum earlier, he knew what his limit was. He wanted his head to stay clear for what he had to do. There was a plan to follow and he was determined to do exactly that.

Rodgers felt the same way. He would later remember that he had a "really small sip [of Everclear] but didn't even touch my blood level at all." Jennifer, though, was different. She quickly drank, multiple shots with Mountain Dew chasers.

"It's better if you mix it," said Rodgers, who had been watching her closely and decided to give her the benefit of his experience. He took back her Mountain Dew and obligingly mixed her a drink. His hand stayed heavy on the Everclear. Then he gave her back the Mountain Dew bottle.

For all of his appeal, Rodgers didn't have any confidence. He knew he was good-looking; he used that. But he also knew he could be a son of a bitch, and if anyone saw that, they wouldn't want a damn thing to do with him. Booze was safer. It guaranteed the result. On cue, Jon drifted away into the canebrake and Rodgers climbed back into the truck.

The Everclear did what alcohol has done for generations. It broke down her defenses and allowed

Rodgers to take advantage of her. Rodgers would later claim that she fellated him first. Rodgers leaned back and enjoyed himself. This was how he had wanted things to start.

After they were done, they continued playing around until Rodgers got hard again. He pulled down her pants. Rodgers would remember that he went inside her and began pounding, pounding, until he came inside her. He claimed the sex was consensual.

On cue, Lawrence came back and leaned up against the side of his truck. Rodgers had had his fun. It was time to go. They all got in and Lawrence gunned the motor. The truck started up, a sharp and rising howl in the dark stillness. It was about 2:00 A.M. Lawrence proceeded back the way they had come, the headlamps picking out the rutted ground, brush and undergrowth, avoiding bad spots as they went.

"Pull over there, Jon," Rodgers shouted.

Lawrence pulled over obediently and stopped. Rodgers turned to Jennifer excitedly.

"You have to see this," he pitched. "There are these pot plants!"

"Pot plants?" Jennifer asked.

"Yes!" and Rodgers got out and walked down the hill to the plants, until he was out of sight. After about a minute, he came running back up.

"They're still there! Come and take a look. I found them awhile ago while I'd been walking around up here."

Jenny decided she needed to see this find.

"Right down there," said Rodgers, pointing off into the darkness.

Rodgers waited until she had just passed him, then reached into his waistband and pulled out the pistol. He followed Jennifer down the hill, ready to shoot her in the back of the head. He picked the gun up to aim and . . . couldn't do it.

Jennifer had gotten to the bottom of the hill. Her senses were clouded by the Everclear; she would have been barely able to stand straight. She may have given a few cursory glances around, but in her drunken stupor it's doubtful she would have really recognized a marijuana plant, let alone a con man.

As they walked back up the hill, Rodgers cleared his mind. Again he raised the pistol, leveled it and aimed. Jennifer was only a few feet from the truck. Once she touched the door handle, that would have meant Rodgers's nerve had run out. She would live and drive home to her mother and her brother and her family and her new postgraduation life as a tank driver or day-care proprietor or whatever she wanted to be.

The pistol discharged with a sharp crack into the night. The bullet entered in the back of her head, over her left ear, and embedded deep in her brain. She sagged, and by the time she hit the ground, her heart had stopped beating.

Shooting her near the truck was not part of the plan. The idea was just to shoot her. Of that, he and Jon had agreed beforehand. But it was a good idea to do it at the top of the hill, in case the body had to be moved. If he'd shot her at the bottom, that would have meant dragging a 145-pound deadweight up a hill, which would leave a lot of evidence if the cops ever found the scene.

Lawrence, whose back had been to Jennifer, turned at the sound of the shot. He saw Jennifer suddenly sitting there on the ground, kind of lying backward. Rodgers was looking down at her. After a while, he looked up with a surprised expression of awe on his face.

"Damn Jon, I got her!"

They bent down and moved Jennifer's body to the back of the truck onto the tailgate. Then Lawrence went to work on her. He took out a knife, which he had carefully packed ahead of time, and cut off her clothes. Stripped naked, with a bullet hole in the back of her head, Jennifer then had her legs sexually spread by Lawrence.

Rodgers walked down toward the creek. When he looked back up, he could see the silhouette of Lawrence in the clearing. It was a full moon and as bright as the time before the sun was completely down. Everything seemed like a dream to Rodgers. He saw Lawrence pull his pants down and shove his erect penis into her dead body.

Rodgers didn't really care for necrophilia; he stayed where he was for a while, watching, until Jon was done. Rodgers walked back up as Lawrence pulled up his pants.

From out of the darkness, they heard a rumbling sound. It was from the other side of the stream but still close by, the unmistakable roar of a boat motor.

"I got a good place where we can bury her," Lawrence said.

Quickly, before anyone on the other side of the river might see what they were doing, they loaded the body into the truck. They were scared—if they were discovered now, that would be it. But no one saw them, no one heard anything.

They drove down the rutted trail until Lawrence stopped at the spot he had chosen. He cut the motor and they stayed in the stillness for a while. A few minutes later, they got out. They kept the headlights on so they could see what they were doing.

Lawrence had sex with the body again.

"Hurry up, hurry up," Rodgers urged.

When Lawrence was done, Rodgers pulled the shovel out from the rear of the truck. It was the same shovel they had already used to dig Justin Livingston's grave. Rodgers moved off a ways and started trying to dig the hole; it was so hard to dig that he got only about six to eight inches deep before he quit. He went back over to the truck just as Lawrence was getting out his scalpel. He also took out a camera and a plastic freezer-type bag.

Back at home, Lawrence had a book on anatomy, *The Incredible Machine*. He had been studying it intently for a while and had circled on the human anatomy chart the lower leg. Lawrence remembered his anatomy now.

Carefully he made his incision at the calf muscle, where it attached to the tendons and bone right underneath the knee. He cut in, going through layers of skin, until he reached the dense muscle and started slicing. The sharpness of the blade aided his labors. The scalpel sliced swiftly through the muscle as Jon pulled it all the way down. He sliced through the connecting tissue at the top and the bottom, releasing the muscle from the fat and skin.

Lawrence stood over the victim. In his bloodied hand, he held the prize. He stuffed it into the Ziploc bag and locked it, then put it into the cooler in the back of his truck.

Rodgers went back to dig the hole, made some progress and quit again. He went in the front of the truck for something and saw on the seat the camera that Lawrence had brought along. Next to it was a Ziploc bag with three packages of Polaroid film. Rodgers took out one of the packages and tore the carton open. He threw it down and then opened the protective wrapping. Once open, he could smell the chemicals of the processing unit built right into the cartridge that he took out and loaded into the camera.

He stood over Jennifer, her lower right leg missing except for bone, and snapped a shot. The picture shot out of the bottom of the camera, but nothing came out; Rodgers had messed it up in some way. He couldn't get it to work; it kept jamming up. Finally it started working. Rodgers began snapping away.

He took picture after picture of the space where her calf muscle used to be. He took pictures of her body. He set up a shot where he placed a knife between her thighs. On film, it looked like a knife really was sticking out of her vagina. Rodgers continued taking pictures of the mutilation, but he wasn't content to be the peeping photographer. Rodgers needed to be more of a participant.

They gathered up Jennifer's clothing, bag, keys. There had been a picture attached to her key chain that had come undone and fallen to the ground. Lawrence bent and looked at it. He recognized who it was instantly. It was a picture of Jenny, but she was a few years younger. Rodgers was not so sentimental. He picked up the picture and the keys and threw them into the woods.

Lawrence put the skin and the fat he had carved from the muscle into a hole near a tree. He covered the hole with dirt and leaves. They looked around and picked up anything they could see, smoothed out any dirt where there might have been blood spatter. Then they got back into the truck. It wouldn't start.

As hard as he tried, Lawrence couldn't get it to turn over. Since they had kept the headlights on, the battery had been run down. The electrical system was finished.

The truck was dead. Having no choice, Rodgers and Lawrence walked through the canebrake under the full moon, the only travelers for miles and miles. They walked five miles, but they were in such good shape, they thought they had walked two. They got to a BP gas station just as the sun was coming up. A bedraggled Rodgers called his girlfriend, Lisa. He needed to get to her before she went to work. Lisa had the early shift at her job. He got her just as she was going out the door.

"Come and get me," Rodgers pleaded.

He shot a woman he had just had sex with. Yet, like any amoral con man, he didn't hesitate to call up his girl for help. Of course, she said "right away." While they waited, Rodgers used the three dollars he started the night out with and another buck Lawrence gave him to buy a pack of cigarettes and two sports drinks.

They relaxed for a while until Lisa showed up at 6:40 P.M. "Where have you been?" Lisa asked urgently. "Why didn't you come home last night?"

"Leave me alone," Rodgers answered. "Shut up. Don't talk to me right now."

But Lisa kept on nagging, right up until the time she dropped them off at Lawrence's house. They got Rodgers's Chevette and drove back up to where Jennifer's body was. Rodgers wasn't sure what he was planning on doing.

Part of him wanted to kill his old buddy Jon Lawrence. Part of him was just lost, having no idea how to proceed. By the time they got back, Rodgers still didn't know what he was going to do.

When they came back, the body was in the same place; no one had been there. Rodgers was driving. He parked right behind Lawrence's truck. Lawrence got out and immediately started bagging her clothes up. Rodgers took more pictures of Jennifer lying where she had fallen after Lawrence had gotten through with her. Before he got to the last few shots, Rodgers decided to do a little cutting of his own.

He took the scalpel and carefully made incisions

on the right and left sides of Jennifer's forehead. Slowly he kept cutting, put the knife down and peeled the scalp up, detaching it from the skull, until it was two flaps of hairy skin pushed halfway up her skull.

Rodgers was satisfied. It would be the final shots. He had her posed the way he wanted, her scalp practically torn from her face, standing up in thick sections of flesh and hair. He snapped a few more shots and watched as the pictures came out and developed.

After he took the last shots, Rodgers saw that Lawrence had already finished the bagging process. The girl's clothes were in two bags. Rodgers put it on top of the hole. Lawrence got some oil and poured it all over the clothes. Rodgers struck a match and burned it. He remembered that he had been smart enough to take the money out of the clothes that she had been carrying—twenty dollars.

And then they went home. The following day, May 9, 1998, Hand arrested Jon Lawrence. Jeremiah Rodgers went on the run.

CHAPTER 9

Years ago, police used to put out an all-points bulletin (APB) when a suspect was wanted. The APB would go out across a statewide and sometimes nationwide network of teletype machines. Later, faxes would be added to the mix along with the basic telephonic and shortwave communication that still forms the foundation of information exchange between law enforcement agencies

With the rapid growth of the Internet through the 1990s, the APB gave way to the be-on-the-lookout-for (BOLO)—instant bulletins conveyed electronically to police department computers nationwide. While the terminology, as well as the technology, may be different, the methodology of the bulletin is the same: be on the lookout for X criminal who may be in your area. The BOLO that the Lake County Sheriff's Office received on May 9 from the Santa Rosa County Sheriff's Office said: "Be on the lookout for Jeremiah Rodgers on suspicion of murder." Since Rodgers had access to Lawrence's arsenal, "subject may be armed and dangerous; approach with caution" was added to the BOLO. It concluded with Rodgers's description.

Police began contacting their snitches in the area with Rodgers's description. Detective Alex Bruck and Sergeant Wendell Garratt met with Lieutenant Stu Schwartz in the Umatilla area of Lake County to discuss the Rodgers BOLO. Schwartz told his detectives that the Rodgers family lived in the area. It was possible Rodgers was trying to reach them. Schwartz gave Bruck and Garratt the fugitive's description and the make and model of the car he had stolen and was thought to still be driving. The detectives hit the streets. Rodgers's father was in town. They decided to pay him a visit.

On the way out to see Rodgers's father, they drove by a downtown bar called Love, Sydney. In the darkened smoky interior, Jeremiah Rodgers was relaxing at the bar. It was a friendly place, where he liked to hang out when he was in town. He knew the owner. Soon Rodgers decided he'd better get going. When he left, another man joined him at the door and they went out together.

Every town has its snitches. The word is still used by police in a derogatory way to describe informers, low-end criminals who can't make it any other way but by informing once in a while on their fellow criminals. And inside Love, Sydney was one of the town's informers who recognized Rodgers. He saw Rodgers leave with "an older white male driving a gold-colored vehicle."

Unlike in the movies, cops don't spend a lot of their time doing surveillance work. It costs a lot of money to put two or more cops in unmarked cars and stake out a location on the chance that something might happen. But when a case is about to break, as this one was, it certainly paid to go the stakeout route, which was how Garratt and Bruck found themselves in an unmarked car staking out Jeremiah Rodgers's father's house.

Nothing happened. After a while, the detectives went across the street and knocked on the front door. They spoke with Rodgers's dad, his stepmother and sister.

"That bar is mine," said Rodgers's dad. "Jeremiah stopped at my bar to have a drink."

Of course, he had done nothing wrong. Rodgers certainly didn't have access to the cop's BOLO on his son.

"I talked to him on the phone," Rodgers said, "and told him to leave. We don't get along."

He told the detectives that Jeremiah had threatened him with harm in the past. Rodgers chipped in with some names of people his son might attempt to contact. The stepmother gave Bruck and Garratt a recent photograph of Rodgers. A short time later, a deputy came out into the field to deliver a photograph taken from the state prison system's on-line public-access database.

It was the mug shot of Jeremiah Rodgers. A quick check back with one of their informants who had knowledge of Rodgers's presence in the county disclosed that he had switched cars. Still preferring to drive Chevys, he was now driving a blue Chevy Corsica. He was spotted on State Road 42.

Bruck and Garratt began driving east on State Road 42. A few minutes later, Rodgers whizzed by at the wheel of the blue Corsica, going in the opposite direction. Garratt turned his car around and hit the gas. The police car shot forward in high-speed pursuit, its eight-cylinder engine humming.

Up ahead, Rodgers had seen the sudden U in his rearview mirror and put the pedal to the metal. Bruck got on the car's retro shortwave and advised police dispatch that they were in hot pursuit of suspected murderer Jeremiah Rodgers.

A marked Umatilla police car received the call. Miles up the road, it sped to a stop at the intersection of State Road 42 and State Road 19. That didn't stop Rodgers. He drove right around the car, leaving some perplexed cops in his wake. He kept going south on State Road 19, not sure where he was going, but just figuring he had to keep going.

Bruck and Garratt ordered Lake County patrol cars to put down Stop Sticks. Stop Sticks are sticks of rubber covered with hollow, pointed tacks used specifically to slow speeding cars. Because the rubberized, lightweight, transportable construction makes them easy to mobilize, the cops had the Stop Sticks completely across State Road 19 almost immediately.

By the time Rodgers saw them, it was too late. The tires passed over them and the front right tire punctured all the way through.

Damn, Jeremiah thought, *damn!*

About a mile farther down the road, the Corsica finally rolled to stop across the center median, a little south of the town of Umatilla. The cops knew Rodgers might be armed, so they didn't approach

Mug shot of
Jon Lawrence.
*(Courtesy of Florida
State Department
of Corrections)*

Mug shot of
Jeremiah Rodgers.
*(Courtesy of Florida
State Department
of Corrections)*

A photo of Lawrence taken shortly after being booked for murder.
(Courtesy of Florida State Attorney's Office)

Jeremiah Rodgers shortly after his arrest.
(Courtesy of Florida State Attorney's Office)

Justin Livingston
as a child,
with his father
Jimmie Livingston, Sr.
*(Courtesy of
Elizabeth Livingston)*

Justin at home.
*(Courtesy of
Elizabeth Livingston)*

Justin's graduation in 1997 from Pace High School.
(Courtesy of Elizabeth Livingston)

Justin at a Hank Williams, Jr. concert in Greenville, Tennessee.
(Courtesy of Elizabeth Livingston)

Elizabeth Livingston, left,
and Diane Robinson,
approximately two weeks
after Jennifer's murder.
(Courtesy of Elizabeth Robinson)

Detective Todd Hand. *(Courtesy of Todd Hand)*

Rodgers and Lawrence cut through this fence to get to Spencer Field, where they murdered Justin. *(Courtesy of Florida State Attorney's Office)*

Police officer points to where the fence was cut and the killers went through with their victim. *(Courtesy of Florida State Attorney's Office)*

The control tower near which Lawrence and Rodgers killed Justin Livingston. *(Courtesy of Florida State Attorney's Office)*

Jennifer Robinson
at age 14.
*(Courtesy of Elizabeth
Robinson)*

Jennifer at
Pace High School.
*(Courtesy of
Elizabeth Robinson)*

Jennifer's
high school
yearbook photos.
*(Courtesy of
Elizabeth Robinson)*

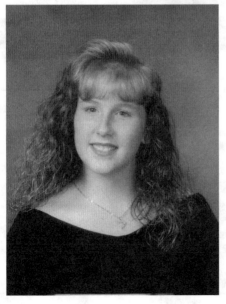

Rodgers's car, which he used the night of the murder to pick up Jennifer and, later, as his getaway vehicle.
(Courtesy of Florida State Attorney's Office)

Lawrence's truck was used to transport Jennifer up to the canebrake where they killed her. *(Courtesy of Florida State Attorney's Office)*

Crime scene markers indicate evidence around the Robinson crime scene. *(Courtesy of Florida State Attorney's Office)*

Close-up of bloody ground where investigators believe the excision of the calf muscle was completed.
(Courtesy of Florida State Attorney's Office)

Justin Livingston's body in the canebrake, as it was first unearthed by the forensic team. *(Courtesy of Florida State Attorney's Office)*

Livingston lying on a white sheet after being extracted from his makeshift grave. *(Courtesy of Florida State Attorney's Office)*

The lower portion of Livingston's body.
(Courtesy of Florida State Attorney's Office)

After Jennifer Robinson was found, investigators took scrapings
from her fingernails to look for evidence.
(Courtesy of Florida State Attorney's Office)

The ruler measures Livingston's grave, about two feet deep.
(Courtesy of Florida State Attorney's Office)

The house in the Lawrence compound where Jon's brother was
accidentally shot. *(Courtesy of Florida State Attorney's Office)*

Evidence photo of Lawrence's dresser.
(Courtesy of Florida State Attorney's Office)

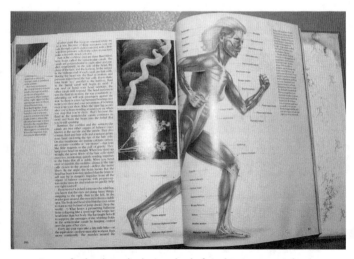

Page of a book on the human body found in Lawrence's home.
(Courtesy of Florida State Attorney's Office)

Jennifer Robinson's calf muscle was found in Lawrence's freezer.
(Courtesy of Florida State Attorney's Office)

Prosecutor John Molchan at his desk in the State Attorney's Office
in Milton, Florida. *(Courtesy of P. Collier)*

Justin's family created this card display for the 21st birthday he didn't get to celebrate. *(Courtesy of Elizabeth Livingston)*

Justin's grave at Strickland Cemetery.
(Courtesy of Elizabeth Livingston)

immediately. Bruck and Garratt arrived to take charge at the scene. They maneuvered their car close to the Corsica, parked and advanced slowly from opposite directions.

Consulting the photograph that his stepmother had given him, Garratt quickly identified Jeremiah Rodgers as the man behind the wheel. He also identified the gun that Rodgers had pointed at his own head as a Lorcin .380.

It was not a bad gambit on Rodgers's part. By acting suicidal, Rodgers forced the cops into a defensive rather than offensive posture. When given a choice, a police officer's innate decency will make him want to save a life rather than take one. Rodgers wasn't sure if the cops would shoot him immediately or not. While standard procedure was not to shoot unless they felt threatened, Rodgers knew that if he was shot and killed, no one would blink.

He figured the cops were after him for killing Jennifer, but he had also helped kill Justin Livingston. Slowly he rolled down his window.

When no one shot him, Rodgers figured he had gotten it right. He appeared to be more of a danger to himself than anyone else. Now it was time to see what he could get for lowering his weapon. It was a negotiation, no different from any business negotiation, except at the end of it, despite all efforts to the contrary, someone could get hurt.

The cops couldn't take a chance of the gun going off accidentally; they had to get him to put it down. And so they started talking. Bruck and Garratt tried to talk Rodgers into throwing the pistol out the window.

"Listen," Rodgers yelled back.

The detectives said they were listening.

"Look, I know about a guy and, uh, a woman too, a girl."

From the BOLO, Bruck and Garratt knew Robinson was wanted for questioning regarding the homicide of a young female. What the hell was he talking about? Had this guy killed a man as well?

"It was out in the forest, in Santa Rosa County. Me and my friend Jon took a girl into the forest on a date."

He was back to talking about the girl again.

"Me and Jon, we took her into the forest after a date. I walked away from the truck."

"Jon shot the girl in the head," Rodgers claimed. "I didn't know he was going to shoot her." Rodgers was pleading with the cops.

Rodgers claimed that he had absolutely, positively no idea what was going to happen. He just figured a little drinking, a little sex, and that would be that for the evening; then that damn Jon . . .

"So I walked away from the truck," Rodgers repeated, "and Jon shot her. I didn't know he was going to do it."

He had no idea that was going to happen. He shouted out to the cops that after Jon shot her, he put the girl's body in back of his pickup truck.

"Then Jon took a scalpel and cut the meat from the girl's leg."

Cops meet strange people all the time in the

course of their work. But discussions with suspects about cutting "the meat from the girl's leg" are rare.

"Jon put the meat from the girl's leg in a plastic bag," Rodgers continued. He figured the worse he made Jon seem, the more it would lessen his own culpability.

"Jon was going to . . . eat it. I helped him bury the body."

From the sound of things, Rodgers had been so scared of the big bad Jon that he had helped him in his unholy work. He was innocent, caught in circumstances beyond his control.

"I want to help put Jon in jail," Rodgers stated, "and I'll help you guys find the bodies because you won't be able to locate them [without me]."

So that was it: Rodgers was angling for a deal, anything to keep himself out of the death chamber.

"I also got some information for you guys about another guy that was shot while sitting in a chair and watching television."

Bruck and Garratt continued their afternoon dialogue with Rodgers. It took a few hours, but at the end of that time, Rodgers had told them enough so that he knew that he was worth more to the cops alive than dead. He felt comfortable enough to lower his gun and surrender.

"Get out of the car and get on the ground with your hands behind your back," the cops ordered.

Rodgers did as he was told. The detectives cuffed him.

"You have the right to remain silent. Anything

you say can and will be used against you in a court of law. You have the right to the presence of an attorney. If you cannot afford one, one will be appointed for you by the court. Do you understand these rights?"

"Yes," Rodgers answered.

It was a routine he was painfully familiar with, and not from watching TV, but from real life. It was time for Rodgers to turn informer.

Criminals turn informer for a variety of reasons. The most common is to save their skins. On rare occasions, it has something to do with a guilty conscience. Sometimes they get a reduced sentence for helping the state prosecute someone else. Rodgers was placed in a squad car and transported to the Lake County Sheriff's Office.

Detective Todd Luce of the Lake County Sheriff's Office called Todd Hand to tell him they got Jeremiah Rodgers. Referring back to the original BOLO on Rodgers, he said they had been in armed pursuit of the suspect. When they finally stopped him with the Stop Sticks, he had "refused to exit the vehicle and held officers at bay for several hours with a .380 pistol." Luce said that during the standoff, Rodgers threw several Polaroid pictures out of the car window and stated, "This is what this is all about" and "I want to get Jon in jail."

While Hand held down the fort, Corporal Mitch Tomlinson and Detective Cliff Armstrong were dispatched to Lake County to bring Rodgers back. The two cops drove down and had a preliminary chat with Rodgers, during which he began revealing some of the details of the murders of Justin Livingston and Jennifer Robinson.

Of course, Rodgers made sure to emphasize Jon's culpability and not his own. He also claimed that the basis for their friendship was that while they were in Chattahoochee, guys were always trying to beat up on Jon.

Rodgers was Jon's protector.

A good detective does not elicit statements using Neanderthal tactics. Once, cops could physically intimidate suspects into confessions and have those confessions stand up under appeal. No more. Even in politically conservative times, judges are bipartisan in their support that statements and confessions must be elicited legally.

Of course, trickery is allowed. So is emotional intimidation. That's how a good cop gets a murder suspect to confess. He develops a nonjudgmental rapport with the suspect in the same way that a therapist does with a patient.

Hand needed to get everything Jon Lawrence said on tape. That would be necessary for a conviction, but the stakes, in a sense, were even higher. He needed to make sure that he persuaded Jon to tell him where Jennifer's body was buried. In addition, there was no apparent motive for the murder, and while motive isn't necessary for a conviction, it helps in convincing a jury.

That evening at 8:50, in the green interrogation room of the Santa Rosa County Sheriff's Office,

Hand once again read Jon Lawrence his rights as he and Joe McCurdy sat down for a conversation.

"Okay, here's a waiver," said Hand, nonchalantly pushing forward a piece of paper attached to a clipboard. "Do you know what a waiver is, Jon?"

"Uh, I think so," Jon answered.

"What's a waiver mean?" Hand asked him.

"Uh, I can't really describe it."

Hand was asking Jon Lawrence to sign a form waiving his constitutional rights to counsel. If he didn't sign it, nothing he said in the interview could be used against him.

"How about if I try to describe it and you can agree or disagree? A waiver is you already know what I've told you, but having in mind what I told you, you still wanna talk to me. Does that make sense to you?" Hand explained.

"All right," Jon answered.

"Okay, it says here, 'have read this statement of my rights shown above and understand what my rights are. I am willing to answer questions and make a statement. I do not want a lawyer at this time. I understand and know what I am doing. No promise or threats have been made to me and no pressure of any kind has been used against me.' Is that true?"

"Yes," Jon answered.

"Okay, I think I'm trying to help you; I just need you to sign that, so we can talk."

Jon signed it.

"Okay, Jon, you signed the statement, is that correct?"

"Yes."

And then he began talking to Jon about Jennifer.

"How could you see her in the dark?"

"'Cause it was a full moon. I remember looking at it."

"Okay, then what happened?"

"I don't remember really too much."

"Did anybody cut her?" Hand said slowly, the anxiety rising a little in his throat. "This is important, Jon; you gotta tell me the truth."

"Yeah, I cut her calf."

Hand asked if he cut from behind her knee down to the back of the ankle.

"Uh, yeah, or more."

"Well, how'd you cut her? What did you use to cut her?"

"A little razor blade. Like the scalpels I have."

Lawrence said he had the scalpels for cutting all different kinds of things. He said he kept them in his truck's toolbox along with bandages for cuts, saws for wood, shovels for digging, rope and a box of surgical gloves.

"Why'd you keep a box of surgical gloves in your toolbox?"

To Hand, the answer was obvious—to commit a crime without leaving prints or DNA. Jon claimed that he used the gloves when he cleaned the entrails of animals. He admitted that he thought he used the gloves when he cut up the victim's calf, but he wasn't sure. Hand knew that forensics would tell for sure.

"Could you show us the general area, Jon, where Jennifer is?" Todd Hand asked.

"It's near the Coon Hill Cemetery. It's on logging roads, down at the Landing."

Too vague.

"If we took you out there, could you show us?"

"I think so. I was real drunk. I can't remember."

"Will you do that now?" Hand requested. "If I drive out, will you show us?"

Jon thought for a second.

"Okay," he answered.

"Okay, do you have anything else to say before we head out?"

"I can't think of anything."

"Did you have anything to do with killing her?" Hand suddenly asked.

"No," Jon answered nonchalantly.

The interview was over and Jon Lawrence was taken back to his cell. Hand sat there for a while, thinking. He could not tell Diane Robinson any of this, of course, until they found the body and identified it, but Hand knew he was close to finding Jennifer Robinson. He also knew that attempting to process a crime scene in the dead of night was not a practical idea. Despite the artificial illumination that the CSTs would bring in, nothing matched daylight.

CHAPTER 10

It wasn't a long drive for Todd Hand and Joe McCurdy from their office—a left turn out of the parking lot, down a few hundred feet of winding blacktop roadway, a left turn through a barbed-wire fence, then pulling up before an ugly building with even more barbed-wire atop stone walls, bars and fences all over the place. It was 8:49 A.M., May 9, when Todd Hand and Joe McCurdy picked Jon Lawrence up at the Santa Rosa County Jail.

"The girl's just up a ways from Blue Springs," said Lawrence as he got in.

He had had time to think and had a better idea where Jennifer was buried. Hand tooled the car out into the county, down deep, dark roads, through the opaque jungle of the Panhandle. Finally they pulled off Ebenezer Church Road in northern Santa Rosa County.

"That way," said Lawrence, pointing down a small fire line off the main road. "Here," Lawrence said, and Hand braked. They got out slowly in a small clearing, Hand putting on his sunglasses; it would be easier to see things in the bright sunshine without squinting.

Hand and McCurdy walked with Jon Lawrence down a rutted trail. They looked off to the side and saw it. It was just a mound of freshly dug dirt in the center of the fire line.

"Over here," said Lawrence.

He pointed down at some ashes. "This is where I burned her clothes," Jon Lawrence said. He took a few steps and pointed at the burial mound. "There's her body."

Hand and McCurdy went back to the car. From the trunk, they extracted yellow tape with CRIME SCENE printed in big black letters. They strung the tape in a large perimeter around the trees that stood like silent sentinels along the fire line.

"Look at that," said Lawrence, pointing at the dirt. "That's Jeremiah's footprint." Hand checked it out. It was a footprint, all right, that would need to be cast for later identification. Hand was too far out into the boonies to use his cell phone, so he called into headquarters on his police radio.

As they were waiting for the forensic specialists and other police to arrive, McCurdy saw a guy driving around the area in an all-terrain vehicle (ATV). They were popular with the kids in the county who liked to explore and camp. The guy, whose name was Lawrence Tierney, said that he was camping in Blue Springs with four of his friends. Blue Springs was just a short walk through the woods.

When McCurdy got to their camp, he saw four juveniles. They had seen and heard nothing the night before. "Pack your belongings and leave the area,"

McCurdy told them. The last thing they needed was kids contaminating the crime scene.

A short while later, the crime specialists arrived. The crime scene, the area directly around the mound of dirt, was photographed from every angle. Evidence markers were placed on the ground next to any evidence that they found. Then it was time to begin digging. Actually, excavating is a better description.

In the distant past, the discovery of a body buried in a shallow grave would bring two husky uniformed cops to the crime scene to start digging. Only when they lifted the body out of the grave would the coroner come in. If that happened today, the detectives would be fired.

Now the CSTs use small trowels to excavate the dirt over the grave. The dirt is placed either on a sheet set up to collect it, or a metal screen. The screen filters out the dirt leaving foreign objects behind.

After gingerly digging down a few feet, the CSTs saw a face begin to appear out of the dirt. The CST's took out fine brushes and began brushing the dirt off Jennifer's face.

Skin that once glowed with health had the unmistakable green pallor of death. It looked like maggots were clogging her eyes, nostrils and mouth. Half her scalp was up over her forehead. The brush continued to gently stroke Jennifer's face, clearing it of the detritus of death.

Insects from the vicinity were gathered up. The idea would be to match what was present at the

scene with the ones that were well along with their
work on Jennifer's body. Soil samples were also
taken.

The CSTs got down on their hands and knees
and scanned the ground. From what Lawrence had
told Hand, they were able to approximate where
the killing took place. Searching that area, they
marked anything they came up with, with a small
yellow evidence marker. Of particular note was a
live round of ammunition collected from the
ground near the left side of Jennifer's makeshift
grave. If it fit a Lorcin .380, they'd have a match to
the alleged murder weapon.

The evidence was collected and put in bags and
carefully marked. Ever since the O.J. Simpson trial,
law enforcement has made a concerted effort to
show a proper, custodial chain of evidence. Otherwise at trial, mistakes could easily lead to an
acquittal. While the CSTs continued to work, Hand,
McCurdy and Lawrence drove a little farther into
the canebrake.

"Over here," said Lawrence. They stopped. "This
is the place where Jennifer was shot."

Lawrence was passive, acquiescent. It was a studied response to authority. He also knew how to
manipulate, to gain sympathy. He began talking
about his and Rodgers's time together in Chattahoochee.

"We'd previously talked about robbing banks and
kidnapping," he said casually. "But we mostly talked
about Dr. Sanguillen at Chattahoochee. Jeremiah

said he wanted to kill Dr. Manolo Sanguillen. Boy, I wish he was here now."

Evidently, Sanguillen and Lawrence had formed a good therapeutic bond.

"Dr. Sanguillen used to lock Jeremiah up a lot. Jeremiah talked about peeling his skin off or cutting him or sewing him back up. Jeremiah said he also wanted to pick people and take them to a cabin and torture them. He wanted to have an underground prison to keep people that he did not like and do weird things to them."

Hand was a rare sort of cop. It wasn't enough to just put the evidence together. He knew that most homicide cases are not "whodunits" but "whydunits." What was the motive and what made Jon Lawrence tick? He really needed to know in order to understand.

"Jon, did someone remove her clothing or was her clothing removed before she was shot?"

"I think her clothes were still on her."

"Who removed her clothing after she was shot?"

"Let's see, Jeremiah took her shirt off and bra off her. I think her pants were already down some, so I uncovered her right leg and just cut her calf off."

There it was again! Lawrence was copping once more to mutilating Jennifer's corpse by cutting the calf muscle out of her body. It was too brutal to be imagined, but he was freely admitting his perversion. As soon as Rodgers's initial statements about Lawrence cutting out the girl's calf muscle were relayed to the police, Hand knew why. It was that moment where everything made sense. He re-

membered the problems Jon Lawrence's mother
had had with her leg. In some sick way, Lawrence
was trying to help her.

What struck Hand, though, was that Lawrence
didn't think there was anything perverted about
it. His tone when describing what he did to her
body was the same as a rational person describing
what they had for lunch yesterday afternoon.

"And what did you do with the clothing?"

"We burned it."

"Why'd you cut [the calf] off?"

"I don't know."

"When you cut it off, what'd you do with it?"

He needed to go over this again. Criminals add
more details every time they repeat their story and
therefore more of the truth.

"I put it in a ZipLoc bag and put it in some ice
and stuck it in a cooler and took it home."

"Why did you take it home?"

Hand knew they had discussed this before. But
he needed to know more.

"To see if it was anything like deer meat."

"You were gonna eat it?" Hand asked, being careful not to show his disgust.

"Yes. We were gonna make two little pieces of
steak and then the other was like deer jerky. Just to
see if it tasted the same."

"Where's the flesh now?" Hand asked.

"In the refrigerator," Lawrence replied.

"The cut on the girl's forehead, how did it get
there?"

"Jeremiah made a little cut on her forehead with

a scalpel. Just to see what the skull part looked like behind her forehead."

Hand remembered a description of one of the pictures Elijah Waldrop had given police.

"Who stuck the knife between Jennifer's legs after she was dead?"

"Jeremiah. He took a picture."

May 11, 1998

Jennifer Robinson had been missing for four days. Her family was still holding out hope, though. Diane Robinson could barely function. Elizabeth Livingston was a little better off and managed to get out of the house to get some air.

"We went up to the Burger King for dinner," Elizabeth recalled, "and, while there, were all set to tack up some new posters of Justin, just like we had before. Only this time, I saw this flyer someone had already put up. There was this picture of the girl, a young girl with flaming red hair. She had come up missing and the last persons she had been seen with were Rodgers and Lawrence.

"I said to a friend, 'Those two are the connection. But where are Justin and Jenny Robinson? What did they do with them?' Normally, my short term memory isn't that good, but I memorized that phone number. When I got home, I dialed it. The person that answered said that the mother couldn't come to the phone then. The police had found a body and they thought it might be Jenny."

Like everything that happened in Pace, Diane found out about her daughter through the grapevine, one person talking to another, the same way Southerners have been doing it for generations.

"Lisa Johnson's mother worked with my sister at a place around here called Vanity Fair for fifteen years," Diane remembered. "My sister went over to Lisa Johnson's house to ask her if she knew what had happened to Jenny. Lisa's mom told her, 'Jenny is dead. They found her body.'

"When she got back, I saw my sister get out of the car. I could tell from her expression what she was going to say, so I turned away. My dad told me my son passed out in the front yard. The shock was too much to handle."

Diane recalled someone telling her that they had found the body and needed help identifying it. It was Detective Janet Philips of the sheriff's department who had gone to the Robinson home to deliver the bad news. She asked if Diane had Jenny's picture to help with identification and if she had any distinguishing marks or scars.

"I immediately thought of the scar on Jenny's leg. When Jenny had been fifteen, her boyfriend had a dog that didn't like her. It was a little bulldog. It bit her on the right calf and left a scar."

Maybe Philips wrote it down, maybe not. Made no difference. Jennifer's right calf no longer existed, except as a pile of meat in a Ziploc bag nestled in Jon Lawrence's freezer.

Hearing the news from Philips that Jenny was

dead, Diane felt like she had been broken into a million pieces. "Jenny was extremely tenderhearted," she said, crying. "You never had to spank her, just get on to her and she'd fall apart. Animals—any stray—she had to feed."

It had taken eighteen hard years to raise her and she had done a damn good job—and just like that, Jennifer was gone. Diane felt pain like she never had in her life. "It's like you are busted in a million pieces. You can't get antibiotics for it. Nothing I can do but take it. The pain is so tremendous."

"At the request of the Santa Rosa County Sheriff's Office under the auspices of the Medical Examiner's Office of the First Judicial District of Florida, an autopsy is performed upon the body identified as Jennifer Robinson," Jenny's autopsy report began.

Jennifer Robinson's autopsy was conducted at Sacred Heart Hospital. The body was photographed from all angles on the slab. What remained of her clothing was taken off and bagged for evidence. So were fingernail clippings, swabs from all her body cavities, scalp and pubic hair samples. The pubic swabs would confirm Jennifer's most recent sexual contact. What wouldn't be clear is which contact took place premortem or postmortem.

She was measured at 5 feet 3 ½ inches and weighed in on the autopsy table at 144 pounds. Perfectly normal. On the other hand, there was the matter of Jenny's scalp. Her fourteen-to-fifteen-inch long, blondish red hair when brushed upward no longer covered what was clearly a postmortem incision to her forehead.

"This is characterized," the autopsy report continued, "by a transverse incision measuring 8 ¾ inches in length which extends to the underlying bony skull."

After she died, Rodgers dug his scalpel into Jenny's forehead. It went in deep enough to impact with her skull. Then came the really grisly stuff.

"A right angle incision up the mid aspect of the frontal region for a distance of 3 ¼ inches is present with an undermining of the skin and reflection of the scalp toward both the left superior and right superior direction."

Rodgers had plunged the knife so deep in her head that Jennifer Robinson's scalp was cut and peeled back over her skull. It was a particularly gruesome piece of mutilation.

Further examination showed "marked postmortem decomposition of the head and face characterized by myiasis." The latter was a nice, clinical way to describe what was really going on. "There is complete destruction of the soft tissue of the eyes."

Maggot larvae had made a home in Jenny's tissues and were eating it up. Regarding the buildup of gases in her body, the report noted that the abdomen was "slightly protuberant. There is a postmortem puncture of the right upper quadrant of the abdomen performed at the scene for body temperature measurement."

Then the medical examiner (ME) Dr. Cumberland, got to the stuff that centered on the lower extremities or legs. Once again, the extensive damage to Jennifer's body, the horrific mutilation yielded to less sensational clinical language.

"The right lower leg is the site of postmortem incision and excision. Extending from just below the knee-cap to just above the ankle from a distance located 6 ¾ inches above the base of the right heel to 19 inches above the right heel, there is a complete excision of skin and skeletal muscle to the underlying tibia and fibula."

Lawrence had done such a good job of cutting out Jennifer's calf muscle that nothing remained from the knee down to the calf, except the two bones that made up that part of the anatomy. As for her upper extremities, ants had scratched her arms and forearms. They had also damaged her back. Jenny, who had taken so much pride in her nails, probably would have been proud that the ME wrote that they were "well manicured."

While the mutilation appeared to be the worst part of the crime, it wasn't, in fact. It was certainly indicative of the criminals' perverse pleasures, but mutilating a corpse or moving it, as they had done in both murders, was actually a relatively minor crime. What was more relevant was the method of death and the cause of death. These are not the same thing.

For instance, if someone threw a blood clot and

died from it, the cause of death would be a blood clot to the brain, but unless the autopsy showed how that blood clot formed and why, then the method of death has to be listed as unknown. In Jennifer's case, the bullet wound was the clincher.

The ME looked at the ⅜-inch-wide gunshot wound behind her left ear. The bullet had traveled into Jennifer's skull, where it was "recovered in the right frontal region of the brain 2 ½ inches below the vertex of the skull and 3 ¼ inches to the right of the midline." What was most telling was the description of the wound track—that is, the way the bullet traveled once it entered the body:

"The gunshot wound track is from back to front, left to right and inferior to superior."

In clinical language, the ME was stating that Jennifer Robinson had been shot from behind. She never knew what hit her. A further examination of the skull showed no evidence of bludgeoning, and further examination of her body showed nothing out of the ordinary. All of her organs were normal. There was no evidence of gunshot wounds or any other physical trauma anywhere else on the body. Most important for any future prosecutions for either Lawrence or Rodgers was this note about her genitalia:

"The vaginal vault is atraumatic."

That meant that there was no evidence that Jennifer had been raped. Whatever sex she had—and it wouldn't be until the vaginal swabs were analyzed that this would be confirmed—was consensual or apparently consensual. The latter could have been the case if she was drugged. A "tox" screen of her blood would tell that tale. Initially, though, it did not appear that, in life anyway, rape was a component of this crime.

"In particular, no evidence of traumatic or foreign body type perforation of the vaginal vault wall is noted."

That meant that the photograph Elijah Waldrop had been shown by Rodgers, of a knife sticking up from Jennifer's vagina, was a posed shot. No one had stabbed her. One of the murderers had simply placed the knife between her thighs. There being no evidence of cuts, the knife was held there simply by pushing her legs together tightly.

"No lesions in the esophagus."

Nobody had stuffed anything down her throat. Killers sometimes get their kicks doing that. The rest of the autopsy proved what Diane Robinson and her family already knew: Jennifer was a healthy girl who should have had a long future ahead of her. It was all there in the autopsy report:

- ✓ The heart weighs 250 grams and has a normal shape.
- ✓ The liver weighs 1545 grams. The capsule is intact.
- ✓ The lungs weigh 735 grams together. The pleural surfaces are deep red-purple in color.

In the end, Jennifer Robinson's death came down to this:

PATHOLOGIC DIAGNOSES:

I. GUNSHOT WOUND TO THE POSTE-RIOR ASPECT OF THE HEAD
  A. INDETERMINATE RANGE PENE-TRATING GUNSHOT WOUND
  B. LACERATION AND CONTUSION OF THE BRAIN
  C. FRACTURE OF THE BASE OF THE SKULL

II. INCIDENTAL FINDINGS
  A. POSTMORTEM DECOMPOSITION—MODERATE
  B. POSTMORTEM INCISION AND RE-FLECTION OF THE FRONTAL REGION OF THE SCALP
  C. POSTMORTEM EXCISION OF THE MUSCULATURE OF THE RIGHT POSTERIOR CALF

EVIDENCE SUBMITTED: HEART'S BLOOD, BLOOD FOR SEROLOGY; FIN-GERNAIL CLIPPINGS; VAGINAL, ORAL AND RECTAL SWABS AND SMEARS; BILAT-ERAL FINGERNAILS; TISSUE; BLOOD FOR TOXICOLOGY

CAUSE OF DEATH: GUNSHOT WOUND TO THE LEFT POSTERIOR SCALP

MANNER OF DEATH: HOMICIDE

Jon Lawrence's actions enabled him to enter a very select category of criminals. In *The Illustrated Book of Sexual Records*, author G.L. Simons cites several cases in which sexual pleasure is derived from cannibalism, including Gilles Garnier and Andrea Bichel, who murdered and mutilated young victims and kept pieces of flesh as a souvenirs.

Jonathan Lawrence fit the definition of a sexual cannibal. It gave him pleasure that he was going to eat Jennifer's calf muscle, whether as a steak or beef jerky. He had deliberately stripped the fat and flesh away so all that was left was the tasty muscle. As for indulging his sudden penchant for having intercourse with a corpse, Lawrence was once again engaging in a rare sexual act—necrophilia.

Jon Lawrence got sexually aroused having sex with a dead body.

According to G.L. Simons, there are only three passages from Grecian antiquity that make reference to necrophilia. Until the middle of the nineteenth century, there was no word to describe the act itself. In 1860, the word "necrophilia" was finally coined by Dr. Joseph Guislain of Ghent. Guislain wrote *Traité sur l'Aliénation Mentale*. A classic text on mental illness, in it he defined necrophilia as the opposite of what a vampire does. Instead of the dead bothering the living, it's the other way around.

Word of the heinous double murder passed across the Florida Panhandle from TV to radio stations, radio stations to newspapers. Reporters worked their sources to find out about this incredibly sensational case in Santa Rosa County, but they were limited by distance and budget.

Unless a story is *really big,* local media don't have the budget to allow their reporters to travel, let alone local media in the Panhandle, one of the state's less affluent areas. And so, the arrests of Rodgers and Lawrence, the modern Leopold and Loeb, went under the radar. Even the Associated Press gave the story little coverage. Perhaps the national media found Lower Alabama, the Redneck Riviera, not worthy of note on the nightly news.

That turned out to be a break for Diane Robinson. She was not inundated with offers to be on *Dateline, 20/20, 48 Hours* or any of the other tabloid TV shows. Amazingly, considering the "cannibalistic" quality to the story, not a line about it appeared in either the *National Enquirer* or the *Star.* Magazines? *Penthouse, Playboy, Maxim,* they all missed it. So the only phone calls and interviews came from local media and, pretty soon, the interest died down.

The bottom line was that the murders might have been the worst thing that could have possibly happened to Santa Rosa. Many a locality that has hosted a sensationalized national murder case has seen business suffer as a result. But fortunately, the county caught a break because the story went under the radar.

And yet with it all, the county and every person in it was shaken to their core by the murders. They were the most horrific crimes in anyone's experience. Perhaps the only thing comparable in the

Panhandle was the depredations of serial killers Ted Bundy and Danny Rolling. Jonathan Lawrence and Jeremiah Rodgers were clearly in that category. Rolling was then on death row; Bundy was dead, having been executed in the electric chair.

Even the state didn't yet know what would happen to Lawrence and Rodgers. Jennifer was now accounted for, but Justin was still missing.

CHAPTER 11

May 11, 1998

Despite the DNA tests used frequently in criminal cases, when a suspect is booked, the first thing the cops do is take his fingerprints. Even in this high-tech generation, it all still starts with the decidedly low tech.

Charles Darwin, the father of modern evolution, actually had a connection to the innovation of fingerprinting. It was Sir Francis Galton, his cousin, who back in 1892 published a book called *Fingerprints*. In it, Galton argued scientifically that fingerprints were unique to every person on the planet. Galton estimated that the odds of fingerprints from two individuals being exactly the same were 1 in 64 billion. He laid out a description of the various pattern types, those distinctive swirls, in each individual's fingerprints. He had been studying fingerprints since 1888.

Galton had made his contribution. He was telling law enforcement all over the world that prints could identify criminals. That still meant the cops had to adapt the technique. Once done, cops used them to catch crooks almost immediately.

A year before Galton published his discovery, Juan Vucetich, an Argentine policeman, in 1891, used Galton's model to create the first fingerprint files in the world. In 1892, Vucetich became the first police officer in history to use fingerprints for the purposes of positively identifying a criminal.

Nine years later, in 1901, England started to use fingerprints to identify criminals. The idea didn't spread to American law enforcement until 1903, when New York State's penal system began to use fingerprints to identify criminals in its prisons. Among them were the legendary Sing Sing [Ossining] and its even more infamous "Big House," which housed the electric chair. The feds caught on in 1904, when they began to use fingerprints at their federal penitentiary in Leavenworth, Kansas.

When Jeremiah Rodgers entered the booking area for Santa Rosa County, his prints were taken just like every other suspected criminal in the past ninety-four years. It was eight o'clock in the morning and Todd Hand was sipping a hot cup of coffee at his desk in the detective squad room.

"Hey, Todd."

He looked up. It was Mitch Tomlinson. They chatted for a few minutes and then Hand went out to meet Jeremiah Rodgers in the jail's booking area. The booking area was a large, windowless room, painted green like the rest of the sheriff's offices.

Rodgers was stiffening up his fingers involuntarily as the cop tried to print him.

"Relax," said the cop taking the print.

The cop rolled the pinkie of his left hand on the fingerprint card, which already had nine of its squares filled up with prints. This was the last. When the cop had finished, he politely handed Rodgers a paper towel to wipe the ink off his hands. Then Todd Hand reread him his Miranda rights.

While the initial Miranda warning is legally enough to make anything a suspect subsequently says admissible, it is just as easy for a suspect to deny ever being issued those rights and claim something to the effect of "Your Honor, I confessed and cooperated under duress." To prevent this from happening, at each stage of the investigative process, detectives are supposed to reissue the Miranda warning.

Todd Hand looked Jeremiah Rodgers over. Rodgers was trying to act cool, detached, but his constantly shifting eyes betrayed his unease. Hand knew that Rodgers had been talking to the Lake County cops. *Let's just see*, Hand thought, *how much cooperation he'll extend to me.*

"Look, Jeremiah, we could use some help here," said Hand, beginning the second round of questioning.

"Sure," Rodgers replied.

"Good. Thanks. I want you to show us where Justin Livingston is."

When Diane Robinson had asked him where Jennifer was, Rodgers had clammed up and feigned ignorance. But that was before his arrest for murdering Jennifer. He had little to fall back on now except his charm, which had gotten him far in the past. Maybe it would get him even further.

As for Hand, it wasn't so much that he was trying to trick Rodgers into a statement. He just had to find Justin. He had a child just like Elizabeth Livingston and Diane Robinson did. He knew how they felt. He couldn't just leave them not knowing the truth.

"I'll help," said Rodgers with a smile. "Let's drive up toward Chumuckla."

Twenty minutes later, Jeremiah Rodgers was sitting in the front seat of a four-passenger unmarked police car. It was a Chevy, his favorite kind of car. Hand drove. In the rear were his partner Joe McCurdy, and Detective Todd Luce from Lake County. After delivering Rodgers, Luce had decided to stick around and see what happened.

Driving slowly through Pace, Hand passed by the Lawrence compound. Hand asked him about possible "evidence locations."

"Jon's toolbox in his truck. Also the abandoned house on the property, especially the last bedroom on the end. There's a .270-caliber rifle, .380 ammunition, two knives and other stuff," Rodgers answered.

Slowly Hand tooled the car up toward Chumuckla.

"How many weapons did you use to kill Justin?" Hand asked.

"Two. Two knives," Rodgers answered.

"Did you guys use rubber gloves?"

"No."

Good, thought Hand, *that means if we recover the knives, their prints will be on them.*

Rodgers answered Hand's questions in that same flat monotone that Lawrence had used to describe Jenny's murder. It was exactly what to expect from a sociopath who has no conscience to contend with.

"When was Justin killed?"

Rodgers thought for a moment.

"Must have been April ninth, around eleven o'clock at night."

"Where?"

"The Spencer Field helicopter landing area."

They had moved the body. That complicated things. If a crime is committed on anything but federal land—county, city, state, town, etc.—the prosecution is handled by the state. There are, however, two ways for federal law to take precedence in a criminal proceeding.

The first way is if the suspect is alleged to have violated federal as opposed to state law. Under ordinary circumstances, murder falls into the category of a state crime, but Rodgers said that Justin had been killed on Spencer Field. That was a federal installation. Any crime that took place on federal property was punishable under federal law.

Actions that violate both state and federal laws may be prosecuted in either or both jurisdictions without violating the constitutional prohibition against double jeopardy. Rodgers and Lawrence were probably looking at federal time if they were convicted for killing Justin, since the action, apparently, was committed on federal land. But right then and there, adjudication was a long way off. First they had to *find* Justin.

Jeremiah Rodgers led Hand and company out into the deepest recesses of the county, out into the canebrake, which whistled softly in the wind. When they got to Sandy Landing, north of Chumuckla, they parked and got out of the car. They made their way down some dusty paths and then suddenly Rodgers stopped and looked down. Hand looked at his watch. It was 10:30 A.M.

"There," said Rodgers, pointing.

To Hand and the others, the mound of dirt looked like a possible grave site. But they couldn't just go digging. That would destroy evidence. They needed to bring in the professionals again. Hand contacted the FDLE and requested that the CSTs come to the site and begin processing what Hand felt certain was their second crime scene—though in order of when the crime actually took place, the first.

One hour and twenty minutes later, at 10:50 A.M., FDLE crime scene investigators Laura Rousseau, John Millard and Chuck Richards, accompanied by the medical examiner Dr. Gary Cumberland, arrived at the scene. After exchanging the usual pleasantries, they went to work.

With Hand and the ME supervising, the CSTs began using the trowels to remove the dirt from what they strongly suspected was the grave of Justin

Livingston. During this process, several articles and pieces of foreign material were discovered by the CSTs. Then they came across a snake skin boot. Digging around it, they saw that it was attached to a leg.

Crime scene technicians began to photograph the grave from every angle. They slowly excavated. There was no hurry, because the victim was dead. As they dug down farther, they took measurements of the grave and the victim's placement in it. Photographs were taken for documentation. The trowels bit into the earth and suddenly the earth began to fall away around Justin's face.

Justin had been in the warm, damp ground for a full month. But rather than having decomposed into some blob of flesh, his face looked instead like some ancient piece of parchment. His eyes were closed; his hair was matted against his skull. The CSTs proceeded to remove any foreign objects from around the body and cataloged them. The excavation continued until they had Justin free from the earth.

To avoid contamination between the victim and the ground, the CSTs placed a white canvas sheet next to the grave. The body was removed and quickly lowered onto the sheet. Briefly the ME examined the body.

The face looked like parchment because partial mummification had taken place. For that to have occurred, the ME knew, the victim had to have been dead for quite a while. Finally the sheet was folded up by the body-removal unit. After the man they figured was Justin Livingston was driven away and taken to Sacred Heart Hospital for autopsy, Hand looked up from the grave, where the CSTs were still working, and saw a commotion.

It was the media. By monitoring the police short-wave frequencies, they had found out that the cops had found another body, the second in two days. They drove quickly to the scene. Video lights cut into the darkness. Pencils hovered over pads, and reporters crowded the police lines. TV journalists were doing standups in front of live TV feeds. Hand looked at them, then over at Rodgers, who was under guard in a police cruiser. Hand walked over and got in.

"We're going," Hand said. He drove through the police lines and past the reporters, who clambered to the side of the car to see who or what was inside. The object of all their attention snoozed quietly in the backseat.

Elbert Lawrence heard that his son was under arrest for murder. Likewise, Elizabeth Livingston learned her son's corpse was found. Maybe it was some primitive urge to see the scene of the crime, to make it real in both their minds. Whatever it was, independently, they got in their cars and drove up to the crime scene in Chumuckla. Cory Liddell, Elizabeth's boyfriend, accompanied her.

When the relatives got there, they ran into each other almost immediately. While the press was off getting interviews with the cops and the forensic experts, Elizabeth squared off with Elbert in the shadows. She glanced over at Cory, who surreptitiously raised his shirt. Nestled underneath, secured by his waistband, was a revolver. If Elbert did anything, he was ready.

Ironically, without even knowing it, the cops were in the middle of a family beef. While they investigated and answered questions for the press, they were oblivious to the drama that might have led to future headlines taking place just a few feet away.

The pent-up emotions of the past few weeks flew from Elizabeth's mouth in a stream of impassioned invective with Elbert the target. She hated this man and she hated his progeny and wanted the Lawrences to disappear off the face of the earth forever.

"I got something to apologize for," she told Elbert. "Your son that blowed his brains out." She was referring to Wesley. "I wish it had been Jon!"

Elizabeth remembered Elbert's face contorting in rage. She knew that Cory had his gun. If Elbert made any move . . . but he didn't. They just exchanged words. Then Elizabeth and Cory walked over to the crime scene itself and saw the hole that Justin had been put into. She finally broke down and Cory helped her back to the car. They got in and drove away. Elizabeth returned to a life that was irretrievably shattered by the murder of her son.

* * *

Fresh from the crime scene, the body was placed on a cold metal examining table at Sacred Heart Hospital's morgue. It was the same hospital Justin had been born in and been taken to for his kidney problems. The hospital had taken care of him on those two occasions and would do so now.

Working with the ME, the CSTs and detectives began the cold, systematic process of stripping the body. The victim's boots, blue jeans, cowboy shirt and underclothes were all taken off and carefully cataloged as evidence. During the process of inventorying the contents of his pants pockets, they found items in his wallet that identified him as Justin Livingston. With the victim stripped down, it was time to begin the actual autopsy with the initial physical examination.

When a person dies, his body begins to decay. Decomposition, or "decomp," as cops call it, happens more quickly in certain parts of the body, like the eyes. Factors like what kind of clothing the victim was wearing at time of death, burial depth, carnivores, humidity, rainfall, temperature and the actual trauma to the body influence the rate of decay.

There is also bacteria to consider. Alive, we can fight most microorganisms. Dead, the body is a breeding ground for bacteria, and they go to work on the tissues immediately. By thirty-six hours maximum, the body begins to smell like rotting flesh; the skin gets more and more greenish red. Gases form in the body cavity and beneath the skin. In some instances, the body explodes from the build-up.

Florida's weather and environment are particularly hard on dead bodies. It makes being an ME in the state a truly challenging experience. With a humid, subtropical climate through much of the state all year, the Gulf Coast's tendency to get hurricanes often, and with abundant, lush tropical vegetation seemingly everyplace, bodies break down immediately.

There was a case down south in Hillsborough County where a serial killer axed to death two women and then threw their bodies in a secluded pond. As reported by Kent Allard in his book *The Mad Chopper,* when the cops found the women two weeks later—and this was in May—the bacteria in the water had eaten away their faces, so there was nothing there to aid in identification. Their skin had literally slipped off their bodies. In Justin's case, likewise, a strange thing had happened. He had been naturally mummified.

According to www.factmonster.com, "natural mummification occurs in favorable soils and climates, particularly cold, arid areas, ice, and peat bogs." The five-hundred-year-old bodies of Inuit women and children had been found intact and frozen in West Greenland.

Once in a while, though, mummification happens in more hospitable climates, where the air and earth cooperate to preserve. While Justin Livingston wasn't that old, considering he had been killed and buried in Florida, the CSTs caught a break.

Justin had been buried in the most rural part of the county. It was a slightly higher elevation, slightly cooler at night and not as humid because it was inland and not directly exposed to the Gulf of Mexico's moist air. While it was understandable when they dug Justin up that he had certainly decomposed some, his body had mummified, slowing down the decomposition so there was a body fit to perform an autopsy on.

After Justin was placed on the slab, his picture was taken from every angle. His fingernails were clipped and placed in plastic evidence bags. After the ME carefully explored his mouth, they took casts of his teeth for identification purposes. They placed clippings of scalp and pubic hairs in evidence bags.

Beginning the physical examination, Dr. Gary Cumberland noted that there was no neck injury, no chest injury, no pelvic or genitalia injuries. Parts of his neck, legs and arms had mummified. However, his back was a different matter.

The coroner's sketch illustrated Justin's wounds from four angles, all on one sheet of paper. For quick, analytical purposes, it's an incredible low-tech tool for understanding a crime. In Justin's case, the sketch was particularly graphic. There were twelve stab wounds across his upper back, in two ragged horizontal lines.

Time to open him up.

Dr. Gary Cumberland used his scalpel to open

up Justin's back. He was going to look inside and see what kind of damage the stabbing had done. Solving a murder is a matter of eliminating possibilities. Establishing extensive, fatal damage from the stab wounds would go a long way toward corroborating Rodgers's story.

Looking through Justin's chest cavity, Cumberland could trace the damage. There were two stab wounds "in the right posterior [rear] chest wall. . . . One stab wound enters the right lung." That was the first stab wound, which Rodgers thought had hit bone and had, instead, hit the lung. It was the force of that blow that brought Justin to his knees and accounted for the wheezing that he displayed as he died.

"The other [wound] goes through the inferior aspect of the right lung, perforates the right hemidiaphragm and extends into the liver for a depth of 1 ½ inches."

That was the second stab wound, the one where Rodgers knelt on the ground next to the critically wounded Justin and finally got up the nerve to stab him again in the back, holding on to the hilt and pushing the blade down, burying it inside Justin's body. The blade had gone more than half a foot inside the chest cavity. It had gone in so deep, it had penetrated the liver.

As for the other ten wounds, "the stab wound track results in perforation of pleural spaces, penetration of both lungs." The left lung had completely collapsed. In the body cavity, Cumberland discovered "a combination of dried fat and dried blood material present in the pleural spaces bilaterally." In other words, Justin had bled internally. Had he not died from the trauma of the stab wounds, he would have eventually bled to death. Justin Livingston never had a chance after the first two stab wounds.

Examination of all the internal organs showed the aforementioned damage to the lungs and liver, but nothing else unusual except for this note under "Urogenital System: The right kidney is surgically absent." At some point prior to his murder, Justin had a kidney surgically removed.

Unless the toxicology report turned up something, it was possible to already say that the victim had died from multiple stab wounds, with the two in the right posterior chest wall being the most fatal. Concluding his autopsy report, Cumberland came to the following conclusions:

PATHOLOGIC DIAGNOSES:

I. TWELVE STAB WOUNDS TO THE POS-
   TERIOR BACK (THREE STAB WOUNDS
   ENTERING THE RIGHT PLEURAL
   SPACE POSTERIORLY).
   A. DEEPEEST MEASURED DEPTH OF
      PENETRATION FROM THE SKIN
      SURFACE IS 6 ½ INCHES.
   B. PENETRATION AND FOCAL PERFO-
      RATION OF BOTH LUNGS AND
      THE RIGHT HEMIDIAPHRAGM
      AND RIGHT LOBE OF LIVER.
II. INCIDENTAL FINDINGS.
   A. STATUS POST RIGHT NEPHREC-
      TOMY

B. MARKED POSTMORTEM DECOM-POSITION
CAUSE OF DEATH: TWELVE STAB WOUNDS TO THE POSTERIOR THORAX
MANNER OF DEATH: HOMICIDE

Hand read over Justin's autopsy report. Under his incidental findings, the doctor had mentioned "nephrectomy." He looked the term up in a medical dictionary: "Nephrectomy—surgical removal of a kidney." It meant that Justin Livingston had only one kidney.

The detective would subsequently find out that Justin had the kidney removed in 1981 because of disease. Because he had only one kidney, he was that much more vulnerable to Rodgers's and Lawrence's assault. Even had the knife missed the liver and hit the kidney, what ordinarily would not be a fatal wound in most people would be fatal in Justin's case, because he had just one. Hand looked at the graduation picture Justin's mother had given him.

The picture was a small, wallet-size shot. It was the picture his mother gave police when Justin had first been reported missing. Looking at it, Hand couldn't tell that Justin was "slow." He had the same smile as any kid being photographed before graduation. Despite his intellectual and emotional problems, Justin had managed to graduate high school, which was no small achievement for a child with his problems.

But with that childlike demeanor, which under ordinary circumstances might just make him the butt of jokes about the mentally retarded, came a childlike innocence. Justin trusted people, just like a child does. Even when he was dying, he still couldn't believe what was happening to him. That he died friendless and alone and was placed in a nameless grave did not inspire hope that in some way his death would be avenged. That his own cousin Jon, who had been his friend his whole life, was the murderer only made it that much more tragic.

For the cop, a basic question remained: Who had done what to Justin Livingston? Rodgers's version of events had them killing him at the copter-landing field in Milton. He admitted to stabbing and suffocating him. But what was Jon Lawrence's part in all of this? Until Hand spoke with Lawrence again, he couldn't be sure.

CHAPTER 12

May 12, 1998, 3:48 P.M.

Jon Lawrence found himself again in the green interrogation room with Hand and McCurdy.

"Okay, Jon, what I want to talk about a little bit today is an incident involving you, Jeremiah Rodgers and Justin Livingston," Hand began casually.

"Tell me a little bit about how you knew Justin?"

"I think he was my cousin," Lawrence answered. "He lived a couple of roads down; he used to come over and see me a lot."

Through patient questioning, Hand established that Justin came to Lawrence's house on the day he disappeared. Around eight or nine, the action began.

"From my house, me and him and Jeremiah rode up to Sandy Landing," Lawrence said. "We drove a pretty good ways up to Chumuckla." Lawrence claimed the purpose of the trip was "to just sit around out there and talk"

Not likely, Hand thought.

"Did Justin plan to go with you from the beginning?"

"He asked if he could ride with us, so he jumped in the back of the truck. I guess he just wanted to ride back there."

"Did you stop anywhere before you got to Sandy Landing?"

"I think we stopped at a Tom Thumb store."

"Why?"

"I wanted to buy some chips, Doritos 3D's style; I always wanted to try some of 'em, so I bought us a bag."

"Justin rode all the way to Sandy Landing?"

"Yeah, he was just sitting up against the tailgate. He didn't really wanna get up front, and it was kind of a long night, still kinda cold."

According to Rodgers, Justin had been killed on the copter field and then they moved the body to a different spot for burial. So, of course, Justin was sitting up against the tailgate and he was cold—he was dead. It would be interesting, Hand figured, to see where Jon Lawrence was going with his account.

"What did you and Jeremiah talk about while y'all were driving out?"

"We didn't really say too much."

"Did Jeremiah talk about Justin on the trip?"

"I don't think he mentioned anything about him."

"What happened when you got to Sandy Landing?"

"We were all standing around out there for a pretty good while, just looking up at the stars. Jeremiah was trying to get him to look up."

"What was the purpose of getting him to look up?"

"I'm not sure, but he just punched him in the chest and told him to lie down."

"What'd he punch him in the chest with?"

"I think just his fist."

Jon Lawrence was telling the truth, a fact borne out by the autopsy report: there was no stab wound to Justin's chest. Rodgers's purpose in getting Justin to look up was to distract him long enough to punch him to the ground without a struggle.

"He told him [Justin] to lay down, that it was just a bad trip, a drug-type thing. 'Lay down and everything will be all right.'"

Justin did lie down on the ground voluntarily. He never expected what was coming. Rodgers deliberately used Justin's innocent nature to hasten his death. Suspecting nothing, he did as Rodgers ordered.

"He [Jeremiah] sounded real nice about it," Lawrence added. "Then Justin, he said, 'Y'all ain't gonna hurt me, are you?' I just told him, 'No, we're just sitting there,' 'cause I wasn't sure what Jeremiah wanted to do."

"Did Jeremiah like Justin?"

"I don't think he did."

He told the cop about how Justin would come over and bug Rodgers for butts and pop. "He [Rodgers] always called him Worm; that was his nickname. And so Jeremiah's been calling him that."

Motive, Hand realized. Rodgers already had the means and, obviously, the opportunity. Here was the motive. He hated Justin. By dehumanizing him, it made it easier for Rodgers to kill him.

"What happened after Justin laid down on the ground?"

"Jeremiah was sitting real close to his left shoulder."

They kept reassuring Justin, who was scared, while they worked up enough nerve to kill him. "Finally I just kept looking down at him and then looked up at the moon."

Suddenly Lawrence laughed.

"And then I looked back down and he [Jeremiah] just raised the knife up real quick and hit him about one or two times in the back, then a couple of times. I was just sitting there; I couldn't really think of what to do."

His cousin is being murdered and he couldn't really think of what to do? How about helping him? Hand wondered.

"It was just kinda like a bad dream," Lawrence continued. "Just sit around and look at the bushes. Then, I guess, when he quit breathing, I went over to get a blanket to cover him up. He looked real kinda cold.

Of course he was. At the moment of death, Justin's body temperature had started to drop as rigor mortis set in. What helped the police to establish that the cause of death was homicide was that the murderers buried the body in the cool earth, which slowed down decomposition, caused partial mummification and preserved body tissues for later examination.

"I just kinda wrapped him up to his chin, where he looked kinda comfortable," said Lawrence.

"Did anybody do anything else to Justin, other than stabbing? Do you remember anything about a shirt being wrapped around his neck?"

"We just sat there for a real long, long time. Oh yeah, that was one of my flannel shirts Jeremiah was wearing, 'cause I had one just like it. He took it off and wrapped it around [Justin's] neck just to make sure he weren't still breathing or suffering."

Evidently, Jon Lawrence did not realize that his cousin Justin was not an animal to be put out of its misery. Nor did he realize that Hand had led him into verbal quicksand with that admission, because while Justin had already been fatally stabbed, Rodgers wasn't satisfied with that bit of cruelty. Rodgers had to smother the poor guy to death to intensify the process. That made the crime particularly heinous, which was going to be of interest to the State's Attorney John Molchan, who would be prosecuting the case.

Lawrence went on to describe how "Jeremiah started digging. He got the shovel out of my toolbox and took his shirt off and was digging real fast."

He described how they picked Justin up and threw him into the makeshift grave and covered him up with dirt. After they had finished their night's labors, they drove "back down to the store and I had a little bit of change left and I bought some Cokes."

"What time was it then?"

"Real late, might have been around three o'clock at night."

"That area around Chumuckla, you know it pretty well?"

"Yeah, I go there every day I can, ever since my dad first showed it to me."

"The knife that Justin was killed with, what happened to it?"

"We took it back to my house or just left it in the truck for a while." Lawrence wasn't sure. "He [Jeremiah] kinda cleaned it off a little bit and put it back in the toolbox and it's been there ever since."

"Did you ever see that knife again after that?"

"Just that time when Jennifer was with us."

"Where'd he clean the knife off?"

"Just where the water is, where the boat ramp is, we stopped there for a while and that's when my truck got stuck. I was trying to back up, got in a sandy spot. So we sat there for a while and built a little fire, cleaning the knife off and just kinda sat there. Finally got the truck out and came on home, was real tired, just dropped him off at Lisa's house. I went home and washed up a little bit and sat in my chair, trying to think of what's happening. Just stayed there all night."

Something bothered Hand. What about Lisa Johnson, Rodgers's girlfriend? What did she know? After they had turned the audiocassette tape over, Hand decided to find out from Lawrence. He asked him if when Rodgers was dropped off, did he see Lisa there? Hand was curious as to what Lisa knew.

"I think she was asleep; she had the doors locked,

so he had to go down to a back window to wake her up."

"Did you see her?"

"I think so; I can't remember."

"Did you take anything from Justin?"

Murderers sometimes trot off with souvenirs of their "victories," but Lawrence "just left him like he was."

"Jon, do you remember the first time I came by to talk to you about Justin?" Hand asked, his voice moving forward slightly with his posture. He stared at Lawrence over the battered table.

"I can't remember."

"The very first time?"

"I forgot."

"Do you remember talking to me on the phone?"

"I don't remember too good."

"Do you remember seeing me?"

"Yeah, I remember you on the phone now."

"Okay, why didn't you tell me [then] what happened? Why didn't you tell me the truth then?"

"I just figured it was a bad dream."

A bad dream with two people in the real world dead, thought Hand.

"You were afraid you were gonna get in trouble for it?"

"I think so."

"Any other reason?"

"I can't think of anything."

Hand could think of a few, like he knew he was guilty of murder. Hand really wanted to nail this guy.

"You were arrested before, right?"

"Uh, for what?" Jon asked, sounding innocent.

"For other things in your past," answered Hand dryly.

"Oh yeah, yes," Jon answered.

"And you went to prison?"

"Yes."

Here it comes. . . .

"And you know the difference between right and wrong?"

"Yes sir."

Bingo!

Insanity is a legal definition that implies that the suspect does not know the difference between right and wrong when he committed the crime he is charged with. It is a defense that can be used in any criminal proceeding where the jurisdiction allows it.

If the suspect does not know the difference between right and wrong, and the defense lawyer can support it, the jury could easily come back with a verdict of not guilty. It is therefore important for cops and prosecutors to prove the opposite—that the suspect knew exactly what he was doing and knows the difference between right and wrong—in order to get a conviction.

When Jon Lawrence admitted to Todd Hand that he knew the difference between right and wrong, he was admitting that he was not legally insane. In so doing, he took one step toward the death chamber.

"Do you think you did anything wrong as far as Justin is concerned?" Hand wondered aloud.

"I just didn't say anything when I should've. I was trying to forget everything."

"Did you plan a story? The story that you told me initially, did you plan that with Jeremiah before I talked to you?"

"I don't know. I just kept telling myself [Justin's] down in a Florida town."

Jon Lawrence was saying that he was living inside a delusion of his own creation, that Justin was still alive someplace else in a Florida town.

"So [Jeremiah] made up a story and you started to believe it yourself?"

"Yes, sir."

"Do you do that a lot?"

Todd Hand was trying to establish a more complete picture of Jon Lawrence's mental state.

"If it's just real bad," Lawrence answered, "if I just can't handle it, I just try to forget about it as best as I can, and then I just get to where I don't believe any of it anymore."

"Jon, have you got anything else you'd like to add to this statement at this time? Go ahead, Jon, if you have something to say."

"I just can't think of anything."

"Anything at all?"

"Well, my head's . . . I can't think."

And the tape recorder was turned off.

CHAPTER 13

May 13, 1998, 2:03 P.M.

The next day it was Rodgers's turn.

"Just the whole story?"

"Yeah, the whole story."

"I can start with whatever?"

"Start with whatever you like," Hand answered gently.

Rodgers had yet to give a full statement about how Jennifer's murder had played out. Hand was curious to hear his version of the events. And so they had gathered once again in the interrogation room.

"Well," Rodgers began, lighting up a cigarette, "when I started meeting Jennifer at the store, she knew me before, but I didn't realize I knew her."

He cleared his throat and went on.

"So it was a few days later that we decided to go out on a date on her free day off from work. We decided to go to a club or a bar in Pensacola, and so the night we were supposed to go out, I met her at the store."

Hand remembered that according to Diane

Robinson, Rodgers only had a few singles in his pocket. That was barely enough for gas to get to Pensacola, let alone to go clubbing. Clearly, he was lying.

"So I followed her home to drop her car off so we could go in mine. I met her mother. And then we left."

They went back to Lawrence's house. They stood around for just a few minutes before deciding to leave. Rodgers noted that Jon Lawrence had already got the liquor, the Everclear. They piled in Lawrence's truck and headed up through the canebrake to Chumuckla.

"Why'd you take Jon's truck instead of your car?" Hand wondered.

"It was easier to go in Jon's truck."

"Why easier?"

"Because it was kind of premeditated, more premeditated than anything Jon had, so we already had that. We piled in his truck and head up toward Blue Springs."

The rest of the story was how Jennifer had gotten drunk on the Everclear and Mountain Dew while Rodgers stayed sober.

"You mix it strong on purpose?"

"Yeah, I gave her like half of the bottle at first in her one-liter Mountain Dew."

Then they started "making out," which led to "consensual sex. Oral sex first and then just straight intercourse." Rodgers was careful to say it was "consensual," lest he be slapped with a rape charge in addition to whatever other trouble he was already in.

After Jennifer and Rodgers were sexually engaged for an hour, in the cab of the truck, Lawrence started sidling over.

"We got out . . . and during that time, Jon's gun was jammed up. He had it then."

"Why was it jammed?"

"It's a piece of shit, it's a .380 and it just jams," said Rodgers.

Lawrence had then whispered to him, "Are you gonna be able to strangle her?"

"No," Rodgers answered. Lawrence then walked into the woods to get the weapon "unjammed."

"Did he let you know when it was unjammed?"

"Yeah, he whispered. He just told me it was ready."

All three got back in the car and were driving out when Rodgers told Jennifer, "There are some pot plants I want to show you."

"Were there?" Hand asked.

"Nah, there was no pot plants."

"Was this part of the plan?"

"To get her out of the truck, yeah. So I walked down the hill first and she didn't get out, so I walked back up and Jon and Jennifer was still sitting in the truck. I asked her, 'Do you wanna look at these before we go?' She said, 'Yeah, I might as well.'"

After she went down the hill and came back, "I cleared my mind. I pulled the gun and I shot her in the back of the head, right where she was almost about to get in the truck." The rest of Rodgers's story made it seem like Jon Lawrence was the mastermind behind disposing of the body and the girl's things. It was after they got home, around dawn, when things started happening fast.

"Jon was gonna try to hose out the back of his truck, but I don't think there was a water hose, so he left."

It was Diane Robinson's friend who had seen Lawrence hosing down his truck and alerted Diane. As for Rodgers, "I went straight home to my girlfriend's house and I went to sleep." When he woke up a few hours later, he got ready to go on the lam. He closed his checking account, went to see his brother, Elijah, showed him the pictures "and then I hauled ass to go down south to see my sister."

Hand, who had been listening intently, was acutely aware that a good defense lawyer at a preliminary hearing would bring up that the statement Rodgers had given was either coerced or said without being properly advised of his rights. But since he'd been arrested, Rodgers had been advised of his rights so many times, he could now recite them by heart.

Hand asked, "Now let me get something straight here. When we started the interview, if you can remember me telling you, the reason we were talking to you was we wanted to talk about Justin Livingston, right?"

"Right," Rodgers agreed.

"And at that point in time you wanted to tell me the truth."

"Yeah, I wanted to tell everything that happened with Justin and Jennifer and the guy that's shot and the drive-by."

"The drive-by?"

There had been no mention of a drive-by shooting before. Many gangs used drive-by shootings as an initiation right. Had Rodgers and Lawrence gotten themselves mixed up with a gang? Had they gotten some sort of exposure to gangs in prison, taken up with them there and then extended their activities when they got out? Hand didn't know, so he kept Rodgers talking.

It seemed that Jon Lawrence had neglected to tell Todd Hand about the actual beginning of their "thrill kill" spree. And since Jeremiah Rodgers was set to talk about a crime that he hadn't as yet been implicated in, let alone charged with, Hand once again gave him his Miranda rights.

With that done, he asked, "Are you doing this of your own free will?"

"Yes," Rodgers answered.

"And why are you doing this, Jeremiah?"

"Because I'm telling everything else that happened and this is one of the last things to tell you. It will make a difference; I just want to tell it."

"Okay," Hand agreed.

Jeremiah Rodgers then told the cop the story of Leighton Smitherman.

March 29, 1998

It should have been just another weeknight for Leighton Smitherman. An elderly man, he was quietly sitting in his living-room chair watching the evening movie with his wife and daughter. Outside his Pace, Florida, home, it was a quiet night in a residential neighborhood not unlike any other in the Florida Panhandle.

There was one thing out of place, however. A truck that no one noticed was cruising the neighborhood. Inside, Rodgers and Lawrence held an impassioned discussion about whom they should kill, who should be their first victim. They kept up their search and kept cruising.

Slowly they drove by a home where they could see the flickering shadows of a TV set on the opposite wall. The window was open and they could make out a man, with his back to them, watching the television. Lawrence, who was driving, pulled off to a secluded side of the Smitherman property.

Rodgers opened the driver-side door of the truck and slowly got out. In his hand was the Lorcin .380 pistol, a cheap automatic weapon that had taken the place of the traditional single-shot Saturday night special. Selling at gun dealers for $138, the Lorcin .380 handgun regularly tops the ATF list of all guns traced to crime.

Smitherman never heard the sharp *click* of the slide being pulled back as the bullet intended to kill him entered the chamber of the gun. He never heard the sharp *crack* as the pistol fired. What Smitherman did hear was the sound of glass shattering and then suddenly he registered pain in his back. The bullet had actually gone through the window, the back of his easy chair and into his neck, where it had lodged.

Rodgers could hear commotion. He didn't stop to see if he had succeeded; there was no time. The cops would be there any minute. He ran back to the truck and got in. "Go," he shouted. Lawrence backed the truck out and drove away like nothing had happened.

Uniformed police from the Santa Rosa County Sheriff's Office arrived at the same time as the ambulance. While the EMTs attended to Smitherman, who was still alive, the cops canvassed the area, which consisted of a series of low-lying houses and trailers. Nobody saw or heard anything out of the ordinary. Unfortunately, the weather had been dry. There were no significant foot or tire prints outside the house, but police did find, on the lawn in front of the house, a shell casing, which they placed in a plastic sleeve for ballistics analysis.

By the time the police had finished their search, Smitherman had been rushed to the hospital. What had started out as a typical night at home watching TV had turned into a nightmare for Leighton Smitherman. Doctors found the bullet inoperable. To remove it would compromise his life. Smitherman would fare better without an operation.

Within a few days, the entry wound had healed over enough that he could be discharged. There was no bandage, just a Band-Aid. Smitherman could thank God that the criminal had used a gun with a small caliber and a bullet that didn't do much damage when it went inside his body. Had the bullet been the kind of dumdum employed by many criminals—a hollow-point bullet, for instance—it would literally have exploded on entry, creating greater tissue damage.

"I hope he's not paralyzed forever," Jeremiah Rodgers said, concluding his account.

Hand was relieved that Rodgers and Lawrence had not gotten involved with a gang. That would have complicated an already complicated case. But it didn't make it any easier that they had shot an innocent man.

"That's everything that did happen. You know, I'm leaving words out, but I honestly can't remember every word that was said. But that's the thing that did happen."

"Okay, I just want to get one more thing straight. Did you bring up the Jennifer topic or did we?"

"I did. On my own."

"Why?"

"'Cause I feel like a piece of shit for what I did [that's why]. I took her life, I ruined her life, her family's life, and after doing all of that, mine don't seem worth as much, so I don't care what happens to me in court. I pray to God I get death row. I honestly do."

Hand had a feeling he might get what he wished for, but he didn't say that. Instead, he asked, "Would you like to say anything to Jennifer's family if you could?"

"To Jennifer's mom, which is the only one that you know I spoke face-to-face with, I just want her to know that I regret so much the decision I made and I'm sorry."

Sorry doesn't bring Jennifer back, thought Hand.

"I wish there was a way I could take it back, which there isn't. The only thing that I can do is tell the whole story and get my punishment. I can get my full punishment and that's the only thing I can change."

Somehow, it sounded more like Jeremiah Rodgers was asking for mercy than admitting to a crime. What he was saying really was not good enough. If the state wanted to get Rodgers in the death chamber, it needed to establish one thing—premeditation.

Premeditation is legally defined as a homicide planned in advance, and is considered more dire than the will to murder, because it persists over a period of time.

"Jeremiah, did you and Jon plan this whole thing out?" Hand asked carefully.

"Yeah."

A good defense lawyer would argue that the things they brought along the night Jennifer was killed might have been used for other purposes. They just happened to be used in the spontaneous act of killing and burying her. What Hand needed to establish for a murder-one indictment was that Jeremiah Rodgers and Jon Lawrence didn't just happen to have the stuff along with which to commit murder, but that they took enough time, beforehand, to plan out the crime and brought that stuff along for that reason.

"The plan was him to shoot her," Rodgers explained, "but however it ended, I'm the one that did it. I can't explain that part; he just didn't do it and I did."

"Did at any point in time, did you or Jon make a list of how you would [kill her]?"

"Jon made a list of the things he would bring."

Hand remembered the list they had confiscated from Jon's house during the search. He smiled inwardly at the thought of being scared by the possum on the floor.

"He kinda planned by hisself when I was at home or wherever I was at, and he showed me the list before we even met up with Jennifer and took her out," Rodgers revealed. "And on the list, as far as I know, was the scalpel, the ice; there was a rope, the knife, I think."

"Camera?"

"Camera."

"Who got the film?"

"Jon did."

"Are there any other pictures other than the ones you had when you turned yourself in?"

Hand was giving Rodgers the benefit of the doubt. He was a fugitive who tried eluding a police dragnet by driving at high speed across an open highway. That hardly qualified as "turning yourself in." But the subsequent Mexican standoff—with armed cops on one side and Rodgers on the other, threatening to commit suicide and then giving up his gun—was enough so Hand could spin the story now so Rodgers had "given up."

"Are there any other pictures?" Hand repeated.

"I had all of 'em." Or so he thought. "I don't know how [Jon] ended up with the ones that were cut up. I don't know how he got those."

"Did you have sex with her after she was dead?"

"No, only when she was alive."

Hand didn't know whether to believe him or not. The truth was, they would never know for sure.

"Do you remember taking a picture of Jon in the woods?"

"No, but I'll be surprised if you tell me there is a picture like that."

"Okay, when we first talked to you today, we told you we wanted to talk about Justin Livingston. Do you have anything you want to say about him?"

"Yeah, if you don't mind."

"Okay, we'll get another tape."

While they were changing cassettes, Hand had a chance to think further. What Rodgers didn't know, because he had little experience with Florida's criminal-justice system, was that admitting to premeditation was the most seriously aggravating factor, more so than the crime itself. Florida's system of criminal justice calls for the trial jury to consider all aggravating and mitigating factors and then recommend life or death to the judge, who then pronounces final sentence. Nine times out of ten, the judge goes with the jury's recommendation.

"The public side of Jon was one of subordination, treated as an inferior, even by his own family," said Hand. "Jon wanted to be acknowledged, respected, powerful. Rodgers was Jon's route to that acknowledgment. With him there to talk and complete the social interaction, Jon could achieve what he had always wanted, to be 'the Man.' Their relationship was symbiotic. Rodgers relied on Jon to do the dirty work and the crazy shit."

That was Hand's operating hypothesis on how the murders were committed. Until he found otherwise, he would go with it.

May 13, 1998, 2:53 P.M.

"Jeremiah, do you recall that we read you your Miranda rights earlier and you signed a waiver to those rights?" Hand began.

Rodgers had signed the waiver before they began talking about Jennifer. Rodgers said that he remembered signing it—Hand didn't need to explain to him like he had with Jon—and agreed to talk "on this particular subject."

"Tell us what you wanted to tell us, and if we have any questions, we'll stop you along the way, but go ahead and tell us what you have to tell us."

If Rodgers knew that the more he talked, the more he was putting his head in a noose, he didn't show it. Hand leaned forward to listen.

"The day all this happened with Justin, me and Jon, everything was on impulse. Nothing was planned at all. We were all sitting around, me, Jon and Justin were sitting around his truck in his yard watching Rick, Jon's brother, and Roy Lee, Jon's uncle, work on Rick's truck. That's when the idea came up between me and Jon to do what happened to Justin."

"What was the conversation like between you regarding Justin?"

"There was no talk, but, you know, the three of us were standing around Jon's truck, he looked at me, and when Justin was looking away, he made a face and took his hand and went across his throat and gave me a questioning eye and I shrugged my shoulders as if I didn't care. Jon knew what it meant; I knew what it meant."

Jeremiah Rodgers had to say it.

"What did you mean?"

"It meant that we were gonna take Justin out and do something to him. That wasn't planned yet."

According to Rodgers, they just took advantage of the situation. It was a spur-of-the-moment thing when he stabbed Justin after they broke into the helicopter-landing field.

"Okay, while he's facing down, and when I got my nerve up, I stabbed him [the second time] between the shoulder blades with the entire blade going through. And I left the knife there for a second and he tried to get up and he got to his hands and knees, so I got up and backed away a little bit with my hand still on the knife."

Then Justin collapsed, and Rodgers pulled the knife out and walked away.

"I turned away from him and I threw the knife down. Jon grabbed the knife."

But Lawrence didn't have the nerve right then to do anything.

"He wouldn't die for a long, long time," Rodgers continued.

"Was he suffering?" Hand asked quietly.

"Yeah, I think so. I didn't have it in me to stab him again. I tried to," but he couldn't. The boy, though, refused to die. "I thought, *it's too late to turn back*. I can't stab him again, so I didn't know what else to do but take my flannel shirt off. I knew he was still alive until I put my shirt around his neck and twisted it to suffocate any air going to him."

"Did you twist it real tight?"

"Tight enough. As tight as I could. And when it got twisted all the way, I kept it in my left hand and I just backed away, and then I looked the other way and I just held it."

He didn't want to see Justin's last moments on earth.

"And I held it for, like, three or four minutes; then I let go. Jon came over and knelt down beside him and stabbed him about seventeen times in the back."

Rodgers then described the whole process of getting rid of the body—from driving the truck through the fence to burying Justin. Hand wanted to know if they ever returned to the grave.

"Yeah, it was a few days to a week later, me and Jon went back out there to see if it'd been messed with. If anybody had found it, and [if] it was the same as when we left it." But everything was the same; no one had discovered Justin's final resting place.

"What did you do with the flannel shirt that was used to strangle Justin?"

"Jon kept that. Jon kept everything. He said he was gonna wash the knives. Said he was gonna wash the shirt. I left everything with him."

"Did you guys have some kind of agreement after you killed Justin as far as what your story was?"

"No, we didn't plan on any questions coming up."

Why should they? They had taken care to bury Justin in a particularly secluded spot. Except for the natural anxiety any murderer has of being discovered, there really was no cause to think that it would actually happen.

"We planned on [Justin's disappearance] being forgotten and that was it."

"Did anyone else other than you two people have any knowledge of you killing Justin?"

"No."

"Is there anything else you can remember about it [that] we may not have talked about?"

"That's beginning to end. Everything that happened, everything exactly," answered Rodgers, sitting back in his chair.

"Do you want to talk about the man sitting in the chair? Would you like to go into that now?"

"Yeah."

They took a break for a few minutes to change tapes. Rodgers had certainly said enough to be charged with murder in the first degree in the death of Jennifer Robinson. Justin Livingston might be another matter.

There were contradictory parts of his statement in reference to Justin's death. He claimed that nothing was planned out, and he claimed that more than once. Yet some of his versions of events seemed to show premeditation.

It would be up to the prosecutor to ultimately determine the charges.

According to ex-wife Diane, Sam Robinson was behind bars at the time of Jennifer's murder.

"The day after Jenny's body was found, he was arrested for a parole violation. He was behind bars. So he called us from jail and said that [law enforcement] would escort him to the funeral if our family paid his expenses. He said he was very anxious to come. Then apparently, he went in front of a judge and the judge allowed him to leave on his own recognizance," Diane remembered.

But Sam Robinson never showed up at his daughter's funeral.

"He never sent cards or flowers."

No, Jenny was buried without her biological father being present. Where he was, no one knows. "I haven't seen him since," Diane continued. As Jenny's coffin was being lowered into the ground, a weeping Diane Robinson promised herself that she would not judge Rodgers and Lawrence for their actions.

There was a trial to come and who knew how it would turn out? No one knows what juries will do, even in cases of murders as heinous as Justin Livingston's and Jenny Robinson's. Still, Diane Robinson was not about to judge them. Let the jury do that. Besides, if she wanted a death sentence and they only got life in prison, then what? Would she be bitter and disappointed the rest of her life?

No, she wasn't going to put herself into that situation. As much as it hurt, she would be realistic. If the jury gave them a life sentence, she would live with that. If they got death, that was even better because they could never get out on the street again and hurt anyone else. But one thing she was never going to be was the mother of the victim who suddenly shows up at the last minute before execution and forgives her daughter's killers.

"If I'm well and alive and they do get executed, I plan to show up for it," said Diane Robinson. "I'm not saying I will watch every minute of their death, but what I am saying is that I will stand there so they can see my face, and as they look at my face, they will think of Jenny. And they will know why they are dying. I just want my presence to stand as silent witness to my daughter's life."

But that wish assumed that both defendants would be convicted. Working in the state's favor was that Florida does not allow a defense of diminished capacity at trial. Therefore, their psychiatric problems could not be used to mount a defense, but they could be used to proffer sympathy from the jury, which sometimes leads to a lesser verdict.

Plus, during the penalty phase, when the jury and judge decided between life and death, all mitigators, the factors in the defendants' life that go toward explaining their actions and behaviors, could be used, including psychiatric background. What it all came down to was, despite the defendants' statements, despite the forensic materials that were being gathered for trial, you just never knew in the end what would happen at trial and sentencing.

PART THREE

CHAPTER 14

May 8, 1998

No one has to tell prosecutors in the state of Florida that if they come across a particularly heinous case of murder, their first job is to figure out if the crime is cold and calculated. If it is, there's a good chance the jury will be death penalty qualified. That means, when the jury is questioned during the voir dire phase prior to trial, they will be asked this question by the prosecutor: "If in the event you find the defendant guilty of murder in the first degree, would you be capable of voting for the death penalty?"

An assent means consideration to be on the jury. A denial means you hit the road. As the chief felony assistant state's attorney of Santa Rosa County, John Molchan had much experience in this phase of the law.

Unlike wealthier counties, like Hillsborough to the south, which takes in Tampa and has a huge modern complex, the state attorney's office for Santa Rosa County is housed in a modest redbrick building, a converted century-old bank, which belies the power of some within to decide life and death.

Molchan's black mustache and black eyebrows give him the sharp good looks of a hero in a film noir. His eyes are just as intensely dark, the kind of guy who wants to see justice done. On the bookcase across from him are pictures of him in an air force flight uniform. He had served, but as a JAG. The flight uniform was just play.

The phone rang and Pat Collier picked it up. She was Molchan's secretary and worked in the connecting office. She instantly knew the voice on the other end of the line. "Hi, honey." It was her husband, Steve Collier, captain of the county's police force.

"It's Steve on line one, John," Pat shouted in.

Next door, Molchan picked up the battered black phone on his desk.

"Hi, Steve, what's up?" said John.

I hope it's just a social call, thought Molchan. It was Friday and things had been unusually busy lately; he could use a weekend off.

"Hi, John. Listen, the Justin Livingston missing-persons case is active. Todd Hand has developed some leads."

A short while later, Hand called Molchan. "He told me this wild story about Polaroid pictures and a girl being murdered." *It always happens on a Friday,* Molchan thought.

On the first floor of the Santa Rosa County State's Attorney's Office, the receptionist is housed in an office behind a large sheet of bulletproof glass. At three o'clock in the afternoon, she looked up. Through her glass partition, she saw Todd Hand walking through the front door. He was accompanied by a guy who couldn't be more than twenty-one. The guy kept his head down. The receptionist recognized Hand and waved him upstairs.

At the top of the stairs, Hand and his charge walked down a narrow corridor, then cut into an office on the right. Pam Collier greeted him. "Hi, Todd, John's waiting for you." She noted the surly-looking fellow by his side. "This is Jon Lawrence," said Hand.

A minute later, Molchan looked up as Hand came through the door. Molchan stood up to his full height of six feet two inches. His broad frame seemed to fill the entire space behind his walnut desk. That's when he saw the young man with Hand was handcuffed. He looked familiar. Hand had the kid wait outside, guarded by a deputy.

Hand took out the cut-up Polaroids and placed them on Molchan's desk. While Lawrence cooled his heels outside, Molchan looked over the pictures and listened to Hand's crazy story. At the end, Molchan sat down and looked out the window, at the Blackwater River. A bridge spanned the river. Beyond that, the area got less and less populated until you were up in the hills.

"Arrest Lawrence as a principal for murder," Molchan finally said. "Take him out to the scene, if you can get him to show you. Oh, Todd, one more thing."

Hand stopped in the doorway.

"What?"

"I know him—Jon Lawrence. I'm the one that put him in jail."

John Molchan had come to Santa Rosa County in 1989. At that time, he was a felony division assistant taking on whatever felony cases his bosses gave him. In 1993, he got assigned the Lawrence "hate crime."

"It was kind of a very strange kind of crime," Molchan remembers. "Jon was one of those individuals you looked at and just wondered what was he about. I treated it very seriously."

Though Jon Lawrence was a juvenile, Molchan pushed for hard time in the state penitentiary. The judge gave it to him. "But I just didn't know what to do with the kid. It troubled me because I knew he was going to get out."

What Molchan saw in Lawrence was a very troubled youth, a young man with hate in his heart, who needed to be isolated from society. Molchan wasn't a social worker; he was a prosecutor. But he was fair. It never occurred to Molchan that he hadn't given Jon Lawrence a chance. If anything, he had actually given Lawrence a chance to surmount his emotional ills.

Despite Chattahoochee's former dicey reputation, it had become a respected institution in treating the mentally ill. Lawrence had undergone therapy and had been medicated; the doctors had tried everything to mediate his psychoses. And they failed.

Molchan never doubted Hand's theory that Rodgers and Lawrence had a symbiotic relationship that enabled them to do together what they could never do alone. From the previous case, he knew Lawrence to be a strange guy: "But I did not at any time think he would do something like *this*."

The prosecutor went back to the other murder case he was working on. Molchan was married with children. Since he only lived two miles away from his office, it was easy for him to get back and forth when he had a particularly busy agenda, as he did that weekend. There was a new shooting that Friday night, where an old man was robbed and shot. On Saturday morning, Molchan had come into the office to begin his paperwork on the shooting when he got a call from Todd Hand.

"We found her," said Hand over the phone. "We found Jennifer Robinson."

Hand said that Lawrence had given a statement and had taken them to the Robinson crime scene. Molchan went out after the CSTs had been given a chance to go through the area. Hand and McCurdy gave him a tour of the crime scene. What Molchan was looking for, though, were not clues to build a case. Rather, the race to get Rodgers and Lawrence into the death chamber had begun.

"I can see things for the death penalty," said Molchan about viewing a crime scene. If the murder looks cold and calculated, serious consideration is given to death. Looking over the crime scene, what struck him was how similarly everyone was reacting. These were professionals. They couldn't look away. They *had* to look.

The death pros—the CSTs, the EMTs, the cops—all of them looked grim; some looked shocked. Even the hardened death pros felt nausea in their stomachs when they saw Jennifer's scalp and how it had been cut back from her skull.

The rest of that weekend passed slowly. Molchan remembered he was at the office all day Saturday and didn't get home till midnight, Sunday morning, May 10. It was Mother's Day, and he had remembered. Though he had wanted to get something better, he had thoughtfully brought home flowers and a card for his wife, who was already asleep. He put them aside and took off his slacks and polo shirt. He was tired and it was hot and humid.

The next day, Sunday, Mother's Day, he took off from work to spend with his family. By Monday, they had Rodgers in custody. As to be expected, he had blamed everything on Lawrence. What had started out as a random shooting, the archetypal random act of violence, had literally turned into a federal case. Since Justin's murder had occurred on naval property, a government reservation, it was a federal crime. Molchan called Michelle Heldmeyer, assistant United States attorney for the Northern District of Florida.

The U.S. attorney is the prosecuting body of the United States Attorney General's Office. U.S. attorneys are assigned to each state to handle federal prosecutions. Because of its vast size, Florida had three of these offices covering the southern, middle and northern districts of Florida. The northern district office is based in Tallahassee. Heldmeyer worked out of the satellite office across the bay in Pensacola. She would take care of the prosecution of Jon Lawrence and Jeremiah Rodgers for the Justin Livingston homicide. Her first decision was whether or not to seek the death penalty.

The attorney general's office decided to indict the duo on capital-murder charges while holding off the decision whether to actually seek the death penalty or not. It just so happened that on January 26, 1998, just a few months before the murder of Justin Livingston, the federal government had implemented changes to its capital-murder statute:

18 USC Sec. 3005

01/26/98

TITLE 18 - CRIMES AND CRIMINAL PROCEDURE

PART II - CRIMINAL PROCEDURE

CHAPTER 201 - GENERAL PROVISIONS

HEADING

Sec. 3005. Counsel and witnesses in capital cases

STATUTE

Whoever is indicted for treason or other capital crime shall be allowed to make his full defense by counsel; and the court before which the defendant is to be tried, or a judge thereof, shall promptly, upon the defendant's request, assign 2 such counsel, of whom at least 1 shall be learned in the law applicable to capital cases, and who shall have free access to the accused at all reasonable hours.

They had been indicted for a capital crime—the murder of Justin Livingston on a federal reservation. Under the new law, Rodgers and Lawrence were guaranteed not one but two attorneys, "one of whom must be learned in the law applicable to capital cases." Therefore, one of the attorneys had to be a death penalty specialist. That only left who got the job to defend them in federal court.

In 1995, the board of directors of the National Association of Criminal Defense Lawyers (NACDL) voted to fund a position of death penalty resource specialist within the highly acclaimed Southern Center for Human Rights. The position's primary responsibility was to coordinate greater involvement of NACDL members in the fight against the death penalty and on behalf of efforts to bring about its abolition.

Part of the resource specialist's responsibilities was to recruit NACDL members to respond to the needs for representation in capital cases at the trial, appellate and postconviction levels. Within the NACDL, this became known as the Federal Death Penalty Resource Counsel Project. It was from this pool of defense attorneys who specialized in death penalty cases that Rodgers's and Lawrence's lawyers for the federal end of their cases would come.

While Heldmeyer and her associates contemplated what to do, Lawrence and Rodgers were about to be split up. Because their statements were contradictory, in which they made the other chiefly responsible for the murders, there was no choice but to try them separately. As to whether or not the state would seek the death penalty, that was left up to the homicide committee in the state's attorney's office in Santa Rosa County. Composed of upper-echelon personnel from that office, including Molchan, they met to consider their decision.

Molchan looked at the initial facts of the case. The notes that Hand and McCurdy had found in Lawrence's home showed that the murder of Jennifer Robinson was premeditated. The list of items Lawrence wrote out that he had to take along with him the night they killed her showed, to Molchan anyway, that Lawrence had made a rational decision to carry out the crime. Rodgers knew all along he was going to be the triggerman; it was no accident that he was the one who happened to lead Jennifer down the hill to see those bogus marijuana plants and then shot her when her back was turned. It was as cold and calculating an action as Molchan had ever seen in his prosecutorial career.

This was cold-blooded murder, mated with mutilation and necrophilia. While the two latter crimes didn't amount to much more than abuse of a corpse, which is a low-level felony, it served to establish a pattern of premeditation and brutality that warranted the maximum penalty the law allowed. Molchan recommended to the panel that they seek death for both defendants.

On the surface, there didn't appear to be any

mitigating circumstances. These were lawyers voting, not psychiatrists, not psychologists, not social workers. They did not consider whatever in the pair's backgrounds drove them to commit these heinous crimes. That was not part of their job. Their job was to enforce the law. And Florida state law clearly stated that what Rodgers and Lawrence were accused of was murder of the most heinous sort.

The homicide panel voted unanimously to seek death.

Prior to trial, Jon Lawrence was examined by Dr. James Larson and Dr. John Bingham. While they found him competent to stand trial, they had some huge caveats. Dr. Larson said of Lawrence that while competent to stand trial, he "does suffer from a mental disease or defect."

More specifically, he diagnosed him as having "(1) Major depressive disorder, recurrent with possible mild psychotic features, in adequate remission, and (2) Personality disorder, not otherwise specified with schizoid and antisocial features." Ominously Larson reported that although "defendant is adequately stabilized at this time, he can be expected to have intermittent bouts of depression, anxiety and suicidal ideation [ideas]."

Dr. Bingham found that Lawrence was experiencing "considerable emotional turmoil and has somewhat of a schizoid and avoidant type of lifestyle (self-isolating, relationships constricted out of fear of criticism and rejection). Although he does not present with [*sic*] any symptoms of psychosis at this time, it is likely that he has experienced brief acute psychotic episodes in the past." If Lawrence suffered from psychotic episodes, that meant that in some way he occasionally broke free of reality.

Lawrence was "marginally able to manifest appropriate courtroom behavior," Bingham continued, "and testify relevantly because he spoke in a barely audible voice, stared at the floor and presented a submissive demeanor. He could not present information in a chronological order, and he suffered from depression and restricted affect."

Jon Lawrence was either an expert deceiver or he really was a schizophrenic barely able, if at all, to stand trial. For its part, the state believed him to be the former.

January 1999

Attorney Denise "Denny" LeBoeuf was appointed as counsel "learned in the law of capital cases" to represent Jeremiah Rodgers in federal court. She would be his death penalty specialist.

Shortly after her appointment, LeBoeuf began to immerse herself in the case. She went down to the sheriff's jail and introduced herself to Rodgers, who was held there. She spent time interviewing him and continued to see him regularly. The latter was essential. She needed to develop the relationship of trust that is so critical in death penalty cases.

It was a race now. While the feds had still not committed to seeking death at trial, they could very easily, and they had a very strong case. The only chance Rodgers had to avoid death, should the government seek it, would be to develop the mitigators that could convince the court to give him life instead. That's why LeBoeuf spent so much time with Rodgers. LeBoeuf began reviewing some four thousand pages of mental health and medical records concerning Rodgers. Finally she began preparing a case budget in order to obtain the expert and investigative resources she would need to prepare the case in mitigation, given her client's history and the circumstances of the offense.

It sounded good on paper. But the court did not approve any of the defense requests for expert and investigative assistance for more than one month after the budget was submitted. When they did finally, on February 23, 1999, it was for what the defense termed "a very limited amount of money."

Still, the money granted was enough for Rodgers's defense to retain Dr. Lee Norton, one of the top mitigation specialists in the country. His job was to discover the mitigators, the factors in Rodgers's background that, through no fault of his own, led him down the path of destruction. If enough mitigators could be found, a judge might have reason to sentence him to life in prison instead of death.

Unfortunately, Norton's investigation was being

curtailed by a deadline——Rodgers was scheduled to go on trial in federal court on March 15. Norton needed more time to develop the mitigators. Without that, Rodgers didn't stand a chance. To help with the case, LeBoeuf had been consulting with Texas attorney Richard H. Burr. In an effort to gain Norton more time, he mounted a pretrial declaration.

"As I have previously informed the Court," he wrote the U.S. District Court for the Northern District of Florida, Pensacola Division, "my practice has been devoted entirely to the trial, appellate, and postconviction representation of defendants in capital cases since 1979."

Because of his experience, Burr had been retained by the Federal Death Penalty Resource Counsel Project as an adviser and consultant to court-appointed and federal defender attorneys engaged in the defense of capital cases in the federal courts. He was working on the Rodgers cases with LeBoeuf. He told the court that Norton found, during his investigation, "facts about extreme physical, psychological and sexual abuse, abandonment, neglect, exposure to inappropriate sexual behavior, and self-loathing that, together, can lead to an understanding of Mr. Rodgers's drive to self-destruct if it is developed fully and followed by appropriate psychological, psychiatric, and neurological evaluation. Once that is understood, it is likely that the connection between Mr. Rodgers's lifelong history of traumatization and the offenses that he is accused of can be understood and presented as powerful mitigation.

"Many mental health and medical practitioners have treated him over the course of his short life. The opinions concerning his behavior have varied widely and have never been based upon accurate and complete knowledge of his psychosocial history. As a result, there has been much misdiagnosis, misunderstanding, and mischaracterization of Mr. Rodgers for much of his life."

It was an eloquent argument, essentially for mercy, before the case had even gone to trial. Burr argued not only for more time for Norton but for LeBoeuf too.

"Ms. LeBoeuf has been required to prepare an extremely complex and difficult case in mitigation, with the assistance of a mitigation specialist in just over four weeks. Since the death penalty was reinstituted in late 1988, no other lawyer in any other federal death penalty case in the country has been required to do this kind of work in such a short period of time."

Back across the bay in the federal building in Pensacola, the U.S. attorney was made aware of the decision by the state to seek the death penalty.

Both the state and federal governments became aware that a conviction on the Livingston murder in federal court would be used as the significant aggravating factor at Rodgers's and Lawrence's state murder trial for killing Jennifer Robinson. In other words, if he was found guilty of the Livingston death in federal court, the state would use that to show that their homicidal rage led to Jennifer's murder and mutilation. They would wind up in the death chamber, which was the ultimate goal.

March 28, 1999

In Richard Burr, Rodgers had one of the best death penalty attorneys in the country. He didn't show up unless there was a real chance a defendant was going to die without his help. Lawrence too had a death-qualified team working for him.

Assistant U.S. Attorney Michelle Heldmeyer made Rodgers and Lawrence the same offer. Plead guilty to killing Justin and she'd take the death penalty off the table. Instead, they would be sentenced to life. Of course, the killers' attorneys knew what the feds were doing. They knew a murder conviction in federal court would be used as a death penalty aggravator in state court. But what choice did they have? They had to take the deal. The whole point was to save the duo from death.

Clad in an orange prison jumpsuit, wearing a passive expression that belied the depravity beneath, Jon Lawrence had come into federal court to enter a plea. The Associated Press reported: "One of two Florida Panhandle men charged with killing two people and burying the bodies in shallow graves has pleaded guilty to murder in one of the cases. Former mental patient Jonathan

Lawrence, 23, of Pace, entered the plea Friday to avoid a death sentence, but he could still face execution if convicted of the other murder."

With his hair cropped close to his scalp, Lawrence had stood with his head bowed in court as he entered his plea. As part of the deal, he had to state before the judge his complicity in the crime.

"I stabbed my cousin Justin," he admitted in court.

In the visitors' gallery, Justin's mother, Elizabeth Livingston, was noticeably absent. She had gone to clean Justin's grave "because he had been tugging at my heart all day long." She said to a reporter who contacted her that she considered Jon Lawrence to be the "devil possessed." It was a comment that Lawrence probably found much to be proud about.

Nothing in Lawrence's plea required him to cooperate in the case against Rodgers. But Rodgers did not know the specifics of Lawrence's deal. His trial in federal court for killing Justin Livingston was supposed to begin on April 5. He subsequently entered a guilty plea too. This is how the federal record reads: "The defendants for the apparently motiveless murder of Justin Livingston on federal property, met while in a state prison mental-health facility. The government's theory is that this was a thrill killing. Rodgers allegedly shot a man through a window a month before in an unrelated killing. All parties are white. Apparently, the United States Attorney did not request permission to seek the death penalty; nevertheless the Attorney General

directed a capital prosecution. Both Lawrence and
Rodgers pled guilty in exchange for the govern-
ment's agreement not to seek the death penalty.
State capital prosecutions are pending."

Just like that, Justin Livingston had found justice
. . . of a sort. It had been just as easy for the feds to
take the plea in exchange for life; why bother seeking death when the state will do it for you? This was
Florida, after all.

Somewhere, Diane Robinson had a dim aware-
ness of what was happening. She might have heard
from somebody that Rodgers and Lawrence were
about to have their cases heard in the federal
courts for killing Justin, but she didn't really care.
Diane Robinson didn't really care about much of
anything anymore. It had been almost a year since
her daughter was murdered and she spent her days
shuffling from couch to bed and back. She had broken down. She was listless, had no appetite, no
desire. She had no idea of whether she would come
out of it, or die too.

CHAPTER 15

If ever two killers seemed bound for the electric chair, it was Nathan Leopold and Richard Loeb. There was such a public outpouring of sympathy toward Bobby Franks's family and a corresponding flow of bile toward Leopold and Loeb, a fair jury would be hard to come by.

The man who showed up in Chicago, in 1924, to try and save the boys' lives had unruly hair, a rumpled jacket, egg-splattered shirt, suspenders and tie askew. He combed his thin gray hair across his forehead, but a cowlick always wound up dropping over one eye. His name was Clarence Darrow.

Since the 1890s, Clarence Darrow had been the country's most prominent defense attorney. He was distinguished not just by his legal brilliance, but by his impassioned defense of things he believed in, such as unions, free speech and civil liberties. It had been Darrow for the underdog, stretching back into the nineteenth century. And here he was in the twentieth, still defending the cases no one else would touch.

Darrow was as clever as he was compassionate. After considering the evidence against his clients,

Darrow formed a plan of attack. He changed their plea from not guilty to guilty. The boys admitted to kidnapping and murder, felony offenses punishable by death under Illinois law. The decision to change the plea was made primarily to prevent the state from getting two opportunities to get a death sentence.

Leopold and Loeb had been charged with kidnapping and murder, both death offenses in Illinois. The state had planned to try the boys on one charge at a time. If they failed to get conviction on the first charge, they would get a second bite of the apple with the second. Darrow decided not to give the state that chance.

Considering Darrow's cleverness, he probably would have found a way to help Rodgers and Lawrence when the federal and state governments coordinated their prosecutions. In the case of Leopold and Loeb, Darrow's entering of the guilty plea meant the case moved automatically to the sentencing phase. Under Illinois law, the death penalty could only be imposed by the presiding judge, John R. Caverly. Darrow felt Caverly was a "kindly and discerning" man. It would be Caverly alone who had to impose the death sentence on the teenagers. Darrow would not let him forget that when he argued for his clients.

Similarly in present-day Florida, despite what a jury votes to do in a capital case, it is always the judge who ultimately imposes the death sentence. In Florida, judges have imposed death sentences on juveniles many times.

Darrow decided to base his defense of the boy's actions by not offering a defense at all, but rather an explanation to show their insanity. If he could show that the boys, because of their insanity, were not responsible for their actions, the judge might have mercy.

The prosecution argued that was nonsense. Psychiatric testimony was only admissible if the defendants claimed insanity during trial. They had offered no such evidence, since they chose to plead guilty. The defense could not then introduce insanity evidence after the fact.

Darrow argued strenuously that evidence of mental disease should be considered as a mitigating factor in consideration of the sentence. In the most critical ruling of the trial, Judge Caverly decided against the state's objection and allowed the psychiatric evidence to be introduced.

Darrow decided to build his case on the backs of four respected psychiatrists who would testify that Leopold and Loeb were insane for a host of reasons. Therefore, they should not be held accountable for their actions.

During the month-long hearing, the state presented more than one hundred witnesses proving—needlessly, in the opinion of many—every element of the crime. The defense presented extensive psychiatric evidence describing the defendants' emotional immaturity, obsessions with crime and Nietzschean philosophy, alcohol abuse, glandular abnormalities, sexual longings and insecurities.

On August 22, 1924, Clarence Darrow began his summation for the defense: "Where responsibility is divided by twelve, it is easy to say 'away with him'; but, Your Honor, if these boys are to hang, you must do it by your cool, premeditated act, without a chance to shift responsibility," Darrow addressed Judge Caverly.

For over twelve hours, Darrow argued that the universe gave us life as "a series of infinite chances." Why should the boys' wealthy background be held against them, any more than their genetic murderous impulses should bring about their deaths at the hands of the executioner?

"Nature is strong and she is pitiless. She works in mysterious ways, and we are her victims. We have not much to do with it ourselves. Nature takes this job in hand, and we only play our parts. In the words of old Omar Khayyám, we are only impotent pieces in the game. . . .

"What had this boy had to do with it?" he argued of Loeb. "He was not his own father; he was not his own mother. All of this was handed to him. He did not surround himself with governesses and wealth. He did not make himself. And yet he is to be compelled to pay."

In defending Leopold, Darrow argued, "Tell me that you can visit the wrath of fate and chance and life and eternity upon a nineteen-year-old boy!"

Darrow had long been an opponent of the death penalty. Once again he attacked it, declaring it "roots back to the beast and the jungle."

A life sentence was punishment severe enough

for the crime. He reminded the judge how little
Leopold and Loeb would have to look forward to
in the long days, months and years ahead: "In all
the endless road you tread there's nothing but the
night."

It was an appeal out of love to the inherent value
in human life. Even Leopold and Loeb had some
value to their lives. When Darrow finally ended his
appeal, tears were streaming down the face of
Judge Caverly and many courtroom spectators.

State's Attorney Robert Crowe closed for the
prosecution. Noting Darrow's reputation, he sar-
castically characterized him as "the distinguished
gentleman whose profession it is to protect murder
in Cook County, and concerning whose health
thieves inquire before they go out and commit a
crime."

Crowe ridiculed Darrow's attempt to excuse the
crime in light of the boys' background and genet-
ics. "My God, if one of them [the defendants] had
a harelip I suppose Darrow would want me to apologize for having them indicted." The "real defense"
in the case was "Clarence Darrow and his peculiar
philosophy of life."

"I wonder now, Nathan," said Crowe, addressing
Leopold directly, "whether you think there is a God
or not. I wonder whether you think it is pure accident that this disciple of Nietzsche's philosophy
dropped his glasses or whether it was an act of Di-
vine Providence to visit upon your miserable
carcasses the wrath of God."

After retiring to consider his verdict, Judge

Caverly came back to the bench two weeks later. "A crime of singular atrocity," was how the judge characterized the murder of Bobby Franks. Yet Caverly cautioned that his "judgment cannot be affected" by the causes of crime. It was "beyond the province of this court" to "predicate ultimate responsibility for human acts."

Caverly pointed out that "the consideration of the age of the defendants" and the possible benefits to criminology that might come about by studying their psyches ultimately persuaded him to spare their lives. "To the offenders, particularly of the type they are, the prolonged years of confinement may well be the severest form of retribution and expiation."

Whether Caverly was referring to the defendants' crime or alleged homosexual preference for one another was never made clear. He didn't elaborate on what he meant by their type. To Darrow, it made no difference—he had won his victory and saved the boys' lives. Would history repeat with the modern-day Leopold and Loeb, Rodgers and Lawrence? Victor Killam sure hoped so.

Killam was the attorney the Florida Supreme Court had assigned to Jon Lawrence's case. Killam took a page out of Darrow's book. He would plead him guilty and try and prove that Lawrence should be given mercy. Prosecutor John Molchan understood. What could he do? There was no defense of diminished capacity in Florida: either you are insane at the time of the crime or you are competent.

"Do you sit there and tell a jury this guy didn't do anything?" Molchan asked. "It becomes a credibility issue with a jury because you're asking them not to sentence him to death."

May 30, 1999

A letter appeared on the editorial page of the Sunday edition of the *Pensacola News Journal*. Under the heading LAWLESS LEADERSHIP, the writer delivered a tirade against President Bill Clinton and his extramarital affair:

> *I am passionately disgusted to live in the most hypocritical, deceiving country God ever allowed to perch itself atop the face of the earth. . . . Move out of this country if I don't like it, you say? I can't. I'm awaiting trial for murder.*
>
> *Jeremiah Rodgers*

Rodgers wrote well, albeit violently—a point noted by the Secret Service, the federal agency that guards the president. They take threats against the president, especially one by a convicted murderer, very seriously. The disposition of the next portion of Rodgers's case interested them.

While Rodgers and Lawrence had received life in prison without parole for killing Justin Livingston, there was always the possibility they could be released at a later date. It had, after all, happened to Nathan Leopold, who was released in 1958 after serving over thirty years. His friend Richad Loeb had died in prison.

Even if Rodgers was convicted for killing Jennifer and received a life sentence, there was still the minute chance he could be released on parole or pardoned by a governor in the distant future. The Secret Service would be watching Rodgers's state murder trial.

Closely.

March 26, 2000

Jon Lawrence came on the docket first.

On March 26, 2000, Jonathan Huey Lawrence pleaded guilty in Judge Kenneth Bell's courtroom to the murder of Jennifer Robinson. A conviction on the murder-one charge was entered and the judge impaneled a seven-man, five-woman circuit court jury for the penalty phase.

Victor Killam had access to the extensive discovery information and had noticed how eloquently Todd Hand and Joe McCurdy had documented the case. Reading between the lines, they clearly had an opinion that Jeremiah Rodgers was the catalyst for the murders. If he could get either McCurdy or Hand to say that under oath in court, it might go a long way toward establishing a mitigating circumstance, and the judge might have mercy and give Jon Lawrence life.

Florida judges create a two-part list. The first part deals with aggravating circumstances. That is where all the reasons for imposing the death penalty are listed. In the second part of the list, mitigating circumstances, the judge lists why it is that the defendant's life should be spared. The idea for a defense counsel, of course, is to tip the list toward the latter. Considering Jon Lawrence's mental history, and despite the fact that a defense based upon diminished capacity was not allowed, Killam felt that he still had a shot at saving Lawrence's life.

March 29, 2000

A jury had gone through the voir dire and had been seated. Having gone immediately to the guilt phase, they were all "death qualified." Now they would hear the evidence that would determine whether Jonathan Lawrence lived or died. "Call Detective Joe McCurdy to the stand," the court clerk said.

McCurdy walked through the slatted wooden divider in the courtroom that separated the visitors' gallery on two sides, into the well of the courtroom, where the judge ruled over the proceedings. On the left side of the room looking forward from the witness stand was the defense table, where Victor Killam and Jon Lawrence sat. On the right was the prosecuting attorney's table, where John Molchan sat with huge folders all around him.

"Do you swear to tell the truth, the whole truth and nothing but the truth, so help you God?"

"I do," McCurdy answered and sat down.

After the usual questions establishing his name and credentials, Molchan took him through the crimes and his investigation, trying to establish once again the defendant's guilt. After he was finished, Killam got up for cross-examination.

"Mr. McCurdy, you talked to both the defendants, did you not?" asked Killam.

"Yes, I did," McCurdy replied.

"Were you able to form an opinion as to who was the leader and who was the follower?"

Molchan spoke up. "Objection, Your Honor. No foundation."

"Sustained," said the judge.

Killam continued his cross-examination. "Based on your conversation with the two of them, were you able to discern who was the person who was making the decisions in this matter?"

Now Molchan got to his feet. "Objection," he shouted. "Lack of foundation, and also this is going beyond the scope of direct examination."

"Absent more of a foundation, I'll sustain the objection."

Killam had been stymied in his strategy. "I'd like the witness on call for tomorrow," Killam said, and let McCurdy go, at least temporarily.

Todd Hand was up next, and Molchan knew that as the chief investigator on the case, Hand clearly had an opinion regarding aspects of Lawrence's personality.

"Judge," Molchan began, "if we could approach on an issue. I understand that they're going to do some cross-examination of Detective Hand. I anticipate—just total anticipation," he said laconically, but added, "I haven't had a chance to talk to counsel, but one of the questions will be, 'Who was the leader, who was the follower?' I mean, we would object to that question on the fact that this is basically an ultimate-issue type of question that's being asked.

"We're going to the ultimate issue that the jury is going to decide as to whether Jeremiah was the dominant person over Jon Lawrence. And our objection is basically from that. There's no question that they can go into words and deeds of those individuals, but to ask him the ultimate issue is, in our opinion, basically objectionable at this point."

Molchan went on to give an example to prove his point.

"A law enforcement officer in a marijuana case, for instance, cannot testify about the amount of the marijuana and whether it's consistent with intent to distribute. And I believe that that falls into the same range of what Detective Hand may be asked in this situation."

Killam, of course, saw things differently and wasn't about to let Molchan win on what was so crucial a decision to the defense, a decision that ultimately could lead to Lawrence's getting death or life.

"Judge, the dynamics of the detective is reading people and determining who the leader is and who is the follower. And [Hand] has got a case file this thick." Killam opened up his arms at least three feet wide. "And he was probably in the presence of both of these defendants more than anybody. And I think we can lay a foundation and he can answer that simple question, if he has an opinion, as to who was the dominant person of those two," Killam argued.

"I'd have to see the foundation and have to hear what the foundation is," the judge answered.

"The foundation would be, 'How much time have you spent with Jon Lawrence? How much time have you spent with Jeremiah Rodgers? Have you taken statements from both defendants? Did you spend time in the car?'"

Killam added: "'Did you compile an extensive file on this case and review that file? Did you give a deposition . . . that lasted from nine in the morning until two-thirty in the afternoon on this issue?' You've been down here a number of weeks. He's the main man to answer that question, as far as none of us have been in the presence of the defendant as much as Mr. Hand. I think he's qualified to answer that question, which one was dominant. It's a thought process he has to pretty much determine before he goes into situations. And you use that dynamic to find the truth, you know, the ol' Mutt-and-Jeff approach."

The judge considered.

"I don't have any problem with the specific facts, or incidences, or things that happened that would go to that; but my question is whether he can give the ultimate conclusion or opinion as a lay witness basically, a lay opinion as to who was the dominant player in this role and that is the ultimate fact. I don't have any question about you being able to ask him, you know, specific facts or questions that would allow you to make the argument to the jury; but the problem is asking him that ultimate question."

It was the ultimate question, wasn't it? Who was more responsible for the death of Jennifer Robinson? Of course, the judge wasn't tipping whether that would make any difference in his mind. For all the lawyers knew, it might not make any difference, anyway, if the judge was inclined to rule that the responsibility for the murder should be equally shared.

"Well, I would submit to the court," said Killam, "the rules of evidence are relaxed; and this opinion is one that he is eminently qualified to make as a detective. And it's inhibiting our right to present mitigating testimony if we're not allowed to ask that question."

"Well, let me think about it a little bit," the judge answered thoughtfully.

Molchan got his last two cents in.

"Our basic [point is] to base it on an ultimate issue for a jury to resolve."

After the state rested, the defense had its chance to plead for Jon Lawrence's life. Just as they were about to do that, they got a break. The judge ruled that, although it would, absolutely without question, be inadmissible in the guilt phase, he would allow primary investigators to opine in this penalty phase "on who was the dominant person."

The judge was taking a courageous stance. He told the hushed courtroom that he could find "no cases on point," that is, precedent for his action, but that he would err on the side of caution in the context of a penalty phase where the "normal scopes and the rules of evidence are relaxed somewhat."

"It's our position that you are asking a layman to give opinions as to the ultimate issue, which is a jury question. I understand the court's ruling. And what the state would ask is that if we find authority, that we be permitted to revisit this issue with the court," asked Molchan.

The judge said they could and reiterated how he struggled with the issue and decided to err "on the side of liberality." Killam stated his position in black and white. "And it's not a layperson that we submit here. We have an expert detective with years of experience and schools involving interviewing techniques, and personalities, and that type of thing. I'm not talking about pulling somebody off the street with no law enforcement experience and asking for that type of opinion. I think to say that he's a layperson is not exactly correct."

It was decidedly unusual for a defense attorney to be arguing the merits of an officer's expertise. They were usually trying to discredit an officer to help their client. Ironically, this was a case where building a detective's credentials up could only help the defense.

Molchan wouldn't give up. He hated the idea of his own witness being used against him, not to mention that it was possible Hand's testimony could establish mitigation. Molchan argued again that it was lay testimony. The judge agreed but said that after "thinking about it hard," the best decision was to admit the testimony.

The judge then took the time to discuss jury instructions and other legal matters for a short while, then adjourned until the next day's testimony.

"Call Detective Todd Hand to the stand," Killam began. Hand came forward, took the oath and took a seat. Killam quickly got Hand to launch into a sampling of his experience.

"I've been to several training schools as to interview and interrogation," Hand testified. "[An interview involves psychology because] when you interview anyone, be it a suspect or a witness or a victim, you have to try to identify where they are coming from, their position, and be able to anticipate what they may say, what they may not say in reference to your investigation."

"And is it helpful to have an opinion about a personality type that you are interviewing?"

"Yes."

"And in very basic terms, do you believe that we have alpha males and beta males?"

"Yes."

"Would you consider Jeremiah Rodgers to be an alpha male?"

"It all depends in what context," Hand warily answered.

He was there to tell the truth, but not to go out of his way to help Killam.

"In relation to Jonathan Lawrence, would you consider [Jon] to be beta and Jeremiah to be alpha?"

"I don't know."

"You spent a lot of time taking statements from Rodgers?"

"Yes."

"Jonathan Lawrence, you spent a lot of time taking statements from him?"

"Yes."

"And based upon the time that you spent taking statements from him and being in their presence, you were unable to form an opinion as to who was the dominant person between the two of them?"

There it was! Hand could appreciate the irony. Everything he accumulated about personality and motive during his investigation, everything he knew to help explain why these characters did what they did, Killam was about to use it to try and save Jon Lawrence's life. And Hand had no choice but to answer truthfully.

"Well, I have an opinion on it, if that's what you want to hear."

No matter how it went, Killam had won his opportunity to present this evidence to the jury.

CHAPTER 16

"Yes. I'd like your opinion," Killam answered earnestly.

"My opinion is in a public forum, I believe, perhaps here, you'll find Jeremiah Rodgers to be the alpha male that you are talking about, gregarious, outgoing, social. In this type of situation, you would find Mr. Lawrence as a quiet, introverted type of individual in an openly public area."

"Well, are you telling me they are different when they are in private, or do you have an opinion on that?"

"My opinion is yes, they are different."

"And how different are they?"

"I believe the biggest difference is in Mr. Lawrence. I think the more I talk to him face-to-face, or one-on-one or two-on-two, he began to open up to me and talk more loud and freely and more relaxed than he did in public when I would confront him, let's say at his residence or in the presence of other people."

"How long did it take you to build the rapport with Jonathan?"

"In hours? Probably two or three."

"What about Mr. Rodgers?"

"One or two. After he was arrested; we're talking postarrest."

Then Killam went for the jugular to prove his point.

"Is it not true, Mr. Hand, that you told me that you felt like there was an alter ego inside of Jonathan Lawrence that Jeremiah Rodgers took advantage of?"

"Yes," Hand acknowledged reluctantly.

"Do you believe that he shot her in the back of the head?"

"Meaning Jeremiah Rodgers?"

"No, Jonathan. Is the evidence unrefuted that Jeremiah Rodgers is the shooter in this case?"

"I believe so."

It was an absolutely brilliant piece of cross-examination. He had established for the first time in court that Jonathan Lawrence had not shot Jennifer Robinson. Victor Killam now had Lawrence holding steady. No longer was he free-falling through the Florida criminal-justice system. He now actually had a chance to make it out alive. Clearly, Killam had established mitigation. He had given the jury an excuse not to send Jon Lawrence to the death chamber, and the excuse was this: someone else had pulled the trigger.

What would they do?

As for John Molchan, he was in a strange situation. Usually on cross-examination, the witness is not very cooperative because it is the defense's witness. But Hand, of course, was different. Molchan knew he could count on Hand not only to be truthful, of course, but to try and help bolster the prosecution's case.

Molchan's cross-examination of Hand elicited testimony that Lawrence initially denied knowing the victim, that in public settings Lawrence was going to be a much more introverted individual, and that Rodgers is a much more extroverted individual.

"You also have an opinion about when they are together?"

"Yes."

"Isn't it true that basically when they combined together, they were working together? Or there was a relationship of some sort that they worked together?"

"I believe that they, when they are in each other's company, they have, I don't want to say equal relationship as far as his calling the shots or whatever, but I believe that Jon Lawrence is much more open and outgoing in front of Jeremiah because of their friendship. Which is only natural."

On redirect, Killam asked Hand, "We were talking [at deposition] about basically the whole chain of events that resulted in this situation that we have before us today: the shooting, the other killing. Didn't you have an opinion that [Lawrence] was following the directions of Mr. Rodgers?"

"I think possibly to a certain extent he may have been, yes," Hand equivocated.

"And did you not make a statement to me that you felt like there was an alter ego in Jonathan

Lawrence? I was seated here [during the deposition] and we were looking at each other dead in the eye and you said that."

"I recall that in detail, but . . ."

"Thank you."

And the defense ended its redirect. Once again, it was the prosecution's turn.

Molchan got Hand to state that Lawrence was not cooperative, that he had a mind of his own and knew what he was doing. Before arresting Lawrence, Hand stated, "He continuously lied." After the arrest, he only "somewhat" cooperated.

"Now, Investigator Hand, you were getting ready to say something to the jury and you had a 'but.' Can you explain your thought process on that, your comment to Mr. Killam?"

"I believe that was a reference to Mr. Lawrence's alter ego. And naturally I'm not a psychologist or sociologist or anything like that, but from my judgment—"

"Then he is not qualified to answer a question," Killam interrupted.

"Overruled," the judge snapped; Killam couldn't have his cake and eat it too. He couldn't question Hand as an expert and then discredit him as not qualified.

"Anyway," Hand continued, "I said something about an alter ego on Jon Lawrence's part, and I believe that he does have an alter ego when he is with Mr. Rodgers. And I believe that the night that Justin Livingston was murdered, and also Jennifer Robinson, I believe that Jon becomes the person that he wanted to be, he always wanted to be and couldn't be in society. And I believe that he becomes very demanding and forceful and violent. And I think that the evidence speaks for itself."

Killam rose.

"Judge, at this time I move the court for a mistrial based upon his testimony."

Killam had fought long and hard and had successfully convinced the court to allow Hand to opine regarding the personalities of Lawrence and Rodgers and how those personalities interacted with each other. Then, after the defense had opened the door to this subject and elicited the testimony it desired on it, they tried to close the door. That could have unfairly left the jury with a misleading impression of the detective's opinion. That is, if the judge agreed with Killam.

"Denied. [Detective Hand], you may step down."

It was during the penalty phase that Jon Lawrence's hallucinations started happening. Victor Killam warned the court that Lawrence was having visual and auditory hallucinations. The judge did nothing other than recessing the penalty phase hearing for fifteen minutes. He did not ask Lawrence about the nature of those hallucinations. Later, Killam told the court that Lawrence was having more hallucinations.

During the second hallucination, the court decided to question Jon Lawrence directly. Excusing the jury, the judge questioned Lawrence, who described being in the field where the murder of Jennifer Robinson occurred. "I don't want to be out there," Lawrence told the court, minus the jury.

The court chose to characterize his hallucination as really "flashbacks, remembering what happened." When pressed, however, Lawrence said the voice on "the tape that I kept hearing in my head" sounded like that of his dead brother, the one who shot himself with the shotgun during the party.

"But you are not hearing other peoples' voices or things that are not replaying?" asked the judge. Lawrence, obviously troubled, merely replied, "I can't really explain it." When pressed again by the court: "Is it a replay of what happened? Is that what is troubling you, or are you hearing other voices?"

Again Lawrence responded ambiguously.

"I don't know for sure."

The judge could have halted the trial if he felt Jon Lawrence was actually hearing voices and therefore was incapable of understanding the charges against him. But he didn't feel that way, and so the case went on. During the penalty phase of Jon Lawrence's trial, every psychologist who testified, or whose report the court considered, noted that he was seriously mentally ill. Dr. Claude Douglas, who performed a 1996 exam to determine if Lawrence qualified for Social Security benefits because of his disability, said:

"The records [from the Florida State Hospital] were quite consistent with what my clinical impressions were when I evaluated [him] back in 1996: That we had a very impaired gentleman. . . . But we have a person who has a significantly impaired sense of reality; impaired in his ability to relate to others; impairment in thoughts and emotions; inability to cope with life's stressors; prone to psychosis and hallucinations. . . . He started experiencing auditory hallucinations at [the time of his younger brother's death], and also command hallucinations that he should commit suicide.

"He has been given every diagnosis in the book that I can find of all the evaluations, including schizoaffective diagnosis, major depression, and bipolar, manic depressive.

"[He had] four or five readmissions to the Crisis Stabilization Unit at Chattahoochee because of suicide attempts and withdraw. And there's also multiple documentation about auditory hallucinations, and would just withdraw, and inability to cope. . . . He will show no emotion whatsoever. And it is like there is nobody home."

Added Douglas:

"I saw no indication in any of the records or history that he initiates anything. . . . I saw no indication in the extensive records that would indicate that he would be a leader. . . . [I]n being withdrawn he becomes needy. In becoming needy he becomes vulnerable."

Among the police records of evidence against Jon Lawrence were two letters they had confiscated from him during their search of his home after Jennifer Robinson's death. In the first, Lawrence wrote:

"You can get free sleeping pills when the nurse

goes by. Yep, the 18ᵗʰ is coming up soon, there's a hole over the doors, a good place for hiding them. The next shower I'll write a new letter."

In the second note found among his possessions, Lawrence hinted at his schizophrenia:

"Me again. I'm hearing voices all the time now like goddamn Aztecs singing. For some reason, they won't shut up. It's a slow beat every two or three seconds. . . . Pretty weird huh?"

Another expert who testified for the defense, Dr. Sam Collins said, "He [Jon] finds himself unable to disagree with others for fear of being criticized and/or rejected. Because he often experiences anxiety when placed in social situations, coupled with his feelings of inadequacy, this man has failed to develop any significant friendships or close friends."

Psychologist Dr. Seth Bennett testified, also for the defense. He said that "[Lawrence] was afraid that that other young man was either going to kill him or steal his truck, and he didn't know what to do, and that he had to go along. . . . I think he was dominated. . . . Certainly a person with that type of brain damage is very easily dominated because of their lack of reasoning and judgment. Withdrawn people easily and routinely fall under the influence of stronger people."

Lawrence was a follower because he was "almost incapable of sustained initiated prolonged activity on his own volition or on his own planning. . . . And so he is vulnerable for that reason to the domination of other people."

Perhaps the most persuasive mitigating testimony came from Jon Lawrence's friends and family. What they laid out for the court was Lawrence's bad childhood that turned into a nightmare adulthood. The Job-like history of the Lawrence family became public knowledge as the testimony from the experts and those who knew Jon Lawrence was delivered. By the eighth grade, Jonathan's IQ had dropped to 78 because of all his travails. His teachers observed him becoming increasingly distant.

In 1990, at age fifteen, Jon started getting in trouble with the law. He was arrested numerous times, primarily for nonviolent offenses and was referred to a psychologist, Dr. Ted Post. Dr. Post found Jon to be in the low average range of intelligence, with borderline-to-low average abilities; he was depressed and confused; he had poor self-esteem; he was learning disabled, causing more frustration and was diagnosed as suffering from the following: conduct disorder undifferentiated type severe, dysthymia, developmental arithmetic disorder, and poor adaptive functioning within the past year.

Finally, in November 1993, Jon went to prison for defacing the church in Pace. On November 17, after being sent to his cell block, he slashed his arm in a suicide attempt. The Department of Corrections reported that he had a history of attempts to commit suicide with "at least fifty suicidal gestures in the past."

Dr. Olga Fernandez diagnosed him as suffering

from adjustment disorder with depressed mood, and antisocial personality disorder. Lawrence remained in the regular prison environment for six months, repeatedly being diagnosed as mentally ill until he was committed to Chattahoochee.

During his year there, he was repeatedly evaluated as being mentally ill and suicidal. The evaluations began to report that he was experiencing intermittent command hallucinations and he was diagnosed as having, among other disorders, schizotypal personality disorder. Schizoaffective disorder is a major mental illness that includes the same hallucinatory features as schizophrenia, with the addition of a serious depression coinciding with the periods of hallucination.

Lawrence returned home after his release from Chattahoochee around August 1995. His mother, Iona, said that he seemed isolated and depressed. He told her then he had been placed on medication in Chattahoochee, but his eyesight suffered and he would not take that medicine anymore. He became paranoid that it would cause him to go blind.

Iona took Jonathan to the Avalon Center of Baptist Health Care, Inc. for psychological help in September 1995. That was where Douglas evaluated him for Social Security benefits. Iona knew her troubled son needed to do something, so she got him into a vocational technical-school program. But he couldn't function there. He lost interest, failed to ask questions and more or less stayed to himself.

Then Iona was hospitalized for her knee surgery

and Lawrence stayed by her side the whole time, only leaving to get a change of clothes. When she got out, Jon took care of her day and night; he was so devoted. Occasionally he did odd jobs around the area, but, for the most part, he stayed in his home, drank and watched movies.

It was while he was in Chattahoochee that Jon Lawrence had made friends with Jeremiah Rodgers. In March 1998, Rodgers showed up at Lawrence's house. He said he'd been having a lot of problems with his girlfriend, Lisa Johnson, and it was an escape for him to go down and sit and watch TV with Jon. That, of course, led to what the defense described as "the crime spree led by Jeremiah Rodgers."

April 7, 2000

Killam had mounted a brilliant defense. He had literally presented to the jury a "how to make a psychopathic killer/mutilator" bible. By showing how the facts of Lawrence's life had led him to his participation in Jennifer's murder, he was trying to take responsibility away from the killer and put it squarely on the shoulders of his background, which he could not control, and society, which did not treat him correctly. If the jury bought the argument, they would have to vote for life in prison.

They didn't. By a vote of eleven to one, the jury recommended death. At the sentencing hearing that followed, Judge Bell had the option of reducing the penalty or going with it.

"This was a senseless, merciless murder," said Bell, who promptly sentenced Jon Lawrence to death, by electrocution or injection, his choice. Lawrence did not show emotion. To anyone who knew him, that was no surprise. Asked after the verdict was rendered if that was enough for her, Diane Robinson said: "Why do I want to lower myself to be on their standards? I made a promise that whatever the jury came back with, I'd accept. But you know, I see all these people who want to run to death row and forgive, but I don't have to forgive them."

July 2000

What could the defense possibly submit as mitigating circumstances in Jeremiah Rodgers's favor? There really was nothing. In the end, the state had been right—it was a no-brainer. Strangely enough, Rodgers got three votes in favor of mercy from his jury. As always, Rodgers had been a con man.

Jeremiah Rodgers had lied, right until the end. Even as he faced his Maker, he continued to lie about what really happened to Justin Livingston. In the ME's postmortem report, it said that Justin was stabbed twelve times.

"Three of the wounds entered the right pleural [lung] space posteriously [from the rear]; nine stab wounds entering the left pleural space posteriously." Both lungs and the liver were stabbed numerous times.

Rodgers claimed the first time he stabbed Justin,

"I tried to stab Justin in his chest, but the knife didn't go through. It just hit his breastbone and the force of that knocked him down."

Not according to the autopsy report, which stated Justin had "twelve stab wounds to the posterior back." Yet there was no stab wound on the front of Justin's body. Jeremiah Rodgers is, therefore, lying. Second, Rodgers said that the second time he stabbed Justin, "I stabbed him between the shoulder blades with all the blade going through."

That could certainly cause massive bleeding. But since both convicted killers agreed that Justin took a long time to die, he certainly didn't seem to be bleeding to death.

Considering that both killers agreed that Rodgers strangled Justin because he just wouldn't die, it therefore seemed likely that the subsequent nine stab wounds were postmortem. Unfortunately, because of the decomposition of the body, and the absence of any trauma to the trachea [breathing tube] or hyoid [throat] bone, which frequently breaks upon strangulation, the ME could not establish that in addition to being stabbed, Justin was smothered or strangled.

Justin Kyle Livingston's death certificate reads "homicide" as "probable manner of death." The "immediate cause of death" is listed as "stab wounds to the back." There is no mention of smothering or strangulation.

EPILOGUE

Jennifer Robinson

To her friends at Pace High School, Jenny didn't die on May 8, 1998, at least literally. They were determined to resurrect her in their yearbook, which was distributed after her death.

At first, it is very confusing, especially considering that most of the dated entries say "5/12/98" and "5/13/98." What makes it even more confusing is that the person the entries are addressed to is dead, and the students writing the inscriptions know that too.

What the class had decided to do for Diane Robinson and her family is give them a signed yearbook from all of Jenny's friends and even some who didn't know her. The idea was to write the entries to Jenny, as if she had survived.

Jennifer:
Hey girl! What's up? Nothing much here, I hope u have a great summer. Remember the good time we had over spring break and on senior skip day (your 18th birthday).

Love,
Laura Dow

That was when Jenny and her friends should have gone to the beach and had a great time— graduating seniors who thought they were indestructible.

Jennifer,
*   You have been a great friend all these years we have been together. Remember Motel 6 on Friday and Saturday. Do not forget Murphy's.*

*   Your friend,*
*   Sandi Ballion*

Jennifer,
*   Hey girl! How's it going? I'm doing ok! I'm just writing to you to tell you that I miss you.*

*   Love always,*
*   Sidney Johnson*

Jennifer,
*   Hey girl. I'm goin' to miss you and I'll always think about you. Oh, remember this, "Friends threw thik and thin."*

*   Friends 4-ever and always,*
*   love ya always,*
*   Justine*

Most were like that, playing the game, going along as if Jenny were still alive, gone away on some trip someplace, maybe to Fort Walton and Disney World. Maybe she was on a shopping trip to New York and would come back loaded with stuffed animals. Or maybe she was just around the corner taking care of some stray that had wandered her way. It was an interesting conceit to make like nothing had happened. But it had, and not everyone who wrote could keep up the facade.

> *You and your family are in my prayers. Being a great person to everyone was a quality I loved, everyone else loved, about you.*
>
> > *Love always,*
> > *Coral Diamonte*

> *Jenny,*
> *I'm so sorry this happened to you! You deserved so much more in life. I'll never forget all the great times we had together. I know we weren't on the best of terms and I'm sorry for that!!! I just can't believe you are gone. . . . We all know that you're in a better place now.*
> *Doris says that she love you and prays for you each and every night. She also prays the guys will never see the light of day again!! The gates of heaven will never spin for them! I love you!*
>
> > *Love always,*
> > *Millie and Doris*

> *Jenny, have a good time in heaven.*
>
> > *Love,*
> > *Susan*

Diane Robinson

Diane Robinson had a breakdown after Jennifer's death. For three years, it was couch to bed to couch. She wasn't able to work. Then one day she woke up and decided it was time for a change. She began a part-time job. She went into grief counseling and began medication.

She said, "If I have to cry, I cry."

One of the ways she chose to cope with her pain was by increasing it.

"I like the physical pain that comes from tattooing," she said. "I put three tattoos on my body. There's a redheaded angel on my right shoulder." That symbolized her daughter, Jennifer, with her always. "The second is a moon lady's face coming out of it. It's on my left shoulder. You can't see it when the hair hangs down over it."

The third one was on Diane's neck. It is an angel's face, with wings and really beautiful hair. The tattoo was in purple ink because "purple was Jenny's favorite color." She talked about a new tattoo she wanted to get along her spine with the names of her children.

"There's nothing I can do," she concluded. "I can either lay down and die or pick up and go on. You have no idea. You have no clue. I had to let go of revenge. . . . I would have given my life for her. . . ."

Diane put up a purple cross where Jenny was killed.

"I went down there the spring after Jenny died.

The river runs across the road. There's a big pond that the river feeds into covered with purple wild-flowers. She was killed on the bank of that little pond. You know, there are still red police [evidence] flags there."

Evidently, the cops hadn't cleaned up completely after processing the crime scene.

"I go up there regularly and think about Jenny."

Elizabeth Livingston

Elizabeth Livingston had a difficult time.

Despite the fact that she had so much tragedy in her family, nothing had prepared her for the loss of her son. While her religious beliefs have helped her survive, revenge had been an overriding thought.

On the first anniversary of Justin's death, Elizabeth had what might be termed a temporary break from reality. The way she recalled it, "I guess I started a riot in the neighborhood."

Elizabeth Livingston spray-painted the corpses of dead dogs red. Then she hung them up on the trees that bordered her front lawn. "I was doing this crazy stuff," she remembered, "and this preacher came down and helped me out."

Like Diane Robinson, she too had a nervous breakdown and was put on medication that has helped her considerably. She too can no longer work at all and has no immediate plans.

"I'm just coping," she said, "and waiting for the day when the men who killed my son are brought into the death chamber at Starke," Florida's prison where executions take place. "I hope me and Diane go see 'em be put down like dogs."

It looks like she will get her wish.

Elijah Waldrop

Elijah Waldrop was devastated by his involvement in his brother's case. "It ruined my whole life," Waldrop told police afterward. "People come in the shop [where he works] and you hear people [gossiping] about them two guys that got arrested. I have to call some of my friends over there to finish the job so I can do something else, 'cause I can't stand hearing about it. I just go to pieces.

"I'm trying to be a man about this, but it don't help none. Not when you knew the people personally. You went to school with 'em and partied with 'em. You talked to 'em on a friend level. I've known Justin ever since we was little kids, ten, eleven years old. And none of this would have happened if I hadn't went and got [Jeremiah] out of jail and brought him up here."

Waldrop thought he was his brother's keeper.

"Them assholes don't know the value of a human life! They don't understand. They don't have no kids. If my brother ever hurt my daughter, I woulda killed him."

Waldrop was just one of many victims of homicide. The ones most people hear about are the dead ones. But the ones that survive—the friends, brothers, sisters, parents—they are victims too.

"I'd paid a price for it. He has no place in none of my family's heart. I have to live the rest of my life with all this in my head. I'll never get rid of it. I hear about it at work. I dream about it in my sleep."

And then Elijah Waldrop thought for a moment and admitted:

"Jeremiah wanted to show me them bodies. I'm glad I didn't now. I'm damn well glad that I didn't, 'cause I'd probably be dead too."

Some adopted children yearn to know their biological family, thinking it would give them some sort of closure to something missing in their adopted family. Ironically, Elijah, who was adopted, had been afforded that closure, but at great price.

"Even though he is my blood brother, he might see it wrong for me turning him in. But I don't think he'd never give up. I think he'd-a went on and he'd-a made it down south and he'd-a killed all my blood family. And that would have been that much more I have to live with the rest of my life.

"Now my daughter's gotta grow up with 'your uncle's a murderer.' I don't want him nowhere around me or my family ever again," Waldrop stated to police.

Todd Hand

Rodgers and Lawrence made Hand look twice at being a cop and the kind of people he came into contact with. Todd Hand was probably the only one with the right idea—he got out of town.

The peripatetic Hand left Santa Rosa County and took a job farther south with the Florida Department of Environmental Conservation. His beat was the Everglades and other state lands, where he tried to make sure they were not polluted by environmental lawbreakers.

Jonathan Lawrence

In March 2003, Jon Lawrence's appeal before the Florida State Supreme Court was turned down. While noting his mental incapacity and neurological problems, the court said he was responsible for his crimes and should be executed, just as the trial court said.

Jeremiah Rodgers

While awaiting execution, Rodgers had once again put his considerable writing skills to good use, advertising on Web sites for pen pals, writing: "I'd like to correspond with a lady-friend, to possibly form a bond of friendship."

That was Jeremiah Rodgers's ad, designed to lure unsuspecting victims into corresponding with a convicted murderer. Whether or not he had responses was not clear. Apparently, it remained his business. Death row prisoners have the right to write as much as anyone else. Unless he committed a crime, he was doing nothing illegal in his advertisement.

Until getting a "fish," Rodgers spent his time waiting for his eventual death. With everyone acknowledging that he was the one who killed Jennifer, despite his denials, of course, there was little or no chance the courts will show him any mercy on appeal. They haven't yet, and there's no reason to think the courts will change their mind.

Author's Note

In over a decade of writing true crime books, I have seen murder of all sorts: by gunshot, knife, bludgeoning, strangling, poisoning and hired contract.

I have seen murderers chop the arms off a victim who lived and murderers deceive everyone from parents to friends to lovers. But the depths of the depravity that Rodgers and Lawrence have shown are the worst I ever seen and caused me to question some long-held beliefs about capital punishment. Even as these words are being written, the debate is still on whether the United States should continue to be the only Western country to endorse capital punishment.

It would be easy to make the argument that Rodgers and Lawrence should be executed for their crimes. Though it wouldn't bring Jennifer or Justin back, it is clear to me that their families are looking forward to some sort of closure by that action. Experience, however, shows me that the families that do the best surviving after one of their own has been killed are the ones who actually let the idea of revenge go.

And yet, as I wrote this book and looked at the

victims in death, and especially in life, I wavered in my conviction that the death penalty was wrong. If two bastards ever deserved to fry, it's these guys. And yet . . .

There is no question of Jonathan Lawrence's complicity in the murders and his depravity. But his neurological background clearly proves that his is a physically defective mind. It is exactly that problem that the Supreme Court has been wrestling with: do we put murderers like Jonathan Lawrence, severely damaged human beings, into the death chamber?

The Supreme Court has said no. I concur.

As for Jeremiah Rodgers, if in the account in this book it seems like I haven't much feeling for him, I tried—I really did. He's just not a very likable guy. Some murderers are; he is not. But he too comes from a damaged background. He too deserves the kind of mercy reserved for society's damaged rejects.

I am just happy that I did not have to judge them. Maybe Diane Robinson has the right idea about that. After Jenny's death, she went to Graceland, Elvis's home, to honor her daughter. She got a little bit of closure there. It doesn't sound like a bad idea.

Fred Rosen
November 2003

A Word About Sources

Nearly every word said by every person in this book is drawn directly from the individuals' recollections. In cases where it wasn't clear what the killers were doing or thinking at a given moment during the actual crimes, I have made a considered journalistic judgment based upon the facts of the case.

As with any homicide, there are sometimes different memories of the same event. In those cases, I have evaluated the competing claims and presented an account based on my judgment of what occurred.

I want to particularly thank Diane Robinson for telling me about her daughter, Jennifer, and Elizabeth Livingston for telling me about her son, Justin. Todd Hand filled in the entire investigation; he was on it from day one to the end. John Molchan took me through the case from then on.

In 1909, Florida passed Chapter 119 of the Florida Statutes. Known as the Public Records Law, it provides that any records made or received by any public agency in the course of its official business are available for inspection, unless specifically exempted by the legislature.

Over the years, the definition of what constitutes public records has come to include not just traditional written documents, such as papers, maps and books, but also tapes, photographs, film, sound recordings and records stored in computers. Throughout the history of Florida's open government, its courts have consistently supported the public's right of access to governmental meetings and records. That includes court and police documents.

Even in the face of such recent public-relations debacles as the portly killer who literally blew up when the electricity hit him, Florida's criminal-justice system has maintained its status as an open-records state, where the average citizen can get court documentation/arrest reports, whatever is needed to understand a criminal prosecution against an individual.

At the heart of this book is the astonishing governmental documentation of the killing and mutilation spree of Jeremiah Rodgers and Jonathan Lawrence. Florida, it should also be added, has the death penalty and uses it. Whether you agree with Florida's death penalty—and I do not—the state's will to maintain an openness to anyone and everyone especially outsiders, is an absolute tribute to the Constitution in these perilous times.

Turn the page for an excerpt
from Fred Rosen's classic
Needle Work,
now available from Pinnacle True Crime.

November 14, 1997

At approximately 1:48 P.M., Deputy Darrin Zudel of the Genesee County Sheriff's Department (GCSD), while working district E-2 in the town of Genesee, Michigan, was dispatched to Fisherman's Park at the northeast corner of Bray and Carpenter Roads. The dispatcher said it was a possible DOA (dead on arrival).

When Zudel got to the park, he found three men and one woman, all in their early twenties. They were the ones who had called in the "911". It seemed that they had gone fishing in the park. On their way to the river, they had discovered a body.

"Stay back," Zudel told them.

Along with two EMTs who had just arrived on the scene, Zudel set out along the path the fishermen had been on only moments before when they made their discovery.

It didn't really look like much, sort of like a package all bundled up in a blanket. Zudel pulled the blanket down from the face and noted that the subject was a woman with blood around the head and also bruising to the face and eyes. He reached down, pulled the blanket aside from her right arm, and put his hand on her right wrist. The body was very, very cold. He was not surprised when he didn't feel any pulse.

Leaving the body with the two EMTs, Zudel went back to his car. By that time, Lieutenant Michael Becker of the Genessee County Sheriff's Department had arrived. Becker had been on uniformed duty when he heard Zudel being summoned and had raced to the scene as fast as he could.

Zudel took Becker back along the trail; Zudel showed him the body. From Becker's preliminary examination, it was clear the woman had been murdered. It was time to bring in a specialist.

Kevin Shanlian was in his office at the Genesee County Sheriff's Department when he, too, heard Central Communication dispatch Zudel's unit to the fishing site located at Bray and Carpenter Roads.

While the park was technically in the township of Genesee, it was located right next to Flint. Flint, Michigan, has one of the highest per capita murder rates in the country. Murders, though, didn't just stop at the city line. They leached over. Unfortunately, homicides were anything but rare in Genesee. Commonplace was a more apt description.

Immediately a question of jurisdiction came up. While the park was in Genesee Township, the township was within the county of the same name.

Therefore, who had jurisdiction? Actually, the answer was both, but the township's police force had two detectives on leave and was understaffed. As a result, they made the practical decision to shift responsibility to the sheriff.

The next call Shanlian heard was from his lieutenant, Michael Becker, summoning him to the scene. The body dump job would be his case. Shanlian reached into his desk.

When he had first started as a rookie, he probably had eight guns on him and a knife in his boot. But the more experience he got, the more he realized how much you used your head on the job. He got to putting the gun in a drawer or in a glove compartment, having to remind himself to take it out when he went into the field.

Now he reached into his desk and took out his 45mm Sig Sauer automatic and snapped it in place in the shoulder holster under his jacket. It was a lot of firepower, but Flint was a high crime area and cops were always one step behind the bad guys when it came to firepower.

He drove quickly to the scene. By the time he got there, the temperature had risen to all of thirty-three degrees, a veritable heat wave in the late Michigan fall.

"She's along that path there," Lieutenant Becker told Shanlian, pointing behind him.

Becker was busy answering half a dozen questions from support personnel. Alone, Shanlian walked along the path and into the park.

The warmer air had mixed with the colder

ground producing a fog that hung low to the earth, swirling around the body of the woman, who looked so warm and comfy wrapped in the flowered blanket that had become her death shroud.

Who was she? How had she gotten there?

Shanlian, a veteran detective at thirty-five, spotted Deputy Zudel, the cop who had first called the homicide in.

"Have the fishermen who discovered the body transported to headquarters, where we'll take their statements. Then go check the trash containers around here and the roadway west of here," Shanlian requested. "Let's see if we can find any evidence that might help us."

Turning to another cop, Officer Pilon, Shanlian asked him to check the trash containers and roadways east of the murder scene. Then he asked Detective Dwayne Cherry to work the death scene as a liaison between the investigating detectives and the Michigan State Police Crime Laboratory out of Bridgeport, Michigan. The latter had been summoned to collect physical evidence at the death scene. It was specifically labeled "death scene," as opposed to "crime scene," because while the body had been discovered there, they didn't know yet where she had been murdered.

He sent a fourth officer back to headquarters to retrieve footwear and a tire impression collection kit. Maybe they'd get lucky and find that the killer or killers had left footprints around the body.

Cops hated body dump jobs. It was like someone just dropped the damn corpse from a plane and then it was the cop's turn to figure out who it was and how it got there. It was a good thing Shanlian had a sense of humor. Otherwise, the body dumps he'd investigated over his sixteen years as a cop would have gotten to him. There were so many, he couldn't count them up even if he had four sets of hands and feet.

Trying to deduce how the killer or killers had dumped the body, Shanlian immediately noted its location in a clearing and the two paths that cut through. Shanlian saw a narrow, maybe two-inch path of what appeared to be burned leaves leading from the parking lot, through the woods, stopping at the asphalt footpath. He went over to view the body and immediately smelled the gasoline on her. He looked back at the burned leaves. Shanlian figured they were trying to burn the body by setting a fuse made out of leaves.

If the flames had actually hit the body, they would have consumed it, throwing the identification process into a more difficult mode than it already was in. The problem for the killer or killers was that the flame went out when the fire hit the asphalt path. This left the body intact, along with hopes of a quick identification.

The cop came back to the death scene with the vehicle impression kit. Assisted by his partner, Chuck Melki, Shanlian made plaster impressions of an unknown vehicle tire impression in the parking lot. The two detectives photographed all the witnesses' and officers' shoe prints that had entered the crime scene. Shanlian also shot all the vehicle tires that had entered the adjacent parking lot. These photographs would later serve to eliminate police and civilian personnel as offering no significance to the commission of the crime.

Up to that point, the victim had remained where she was, no more than an insignificant part of the landscape. Now she became an active participant in her own murder investigation.

Taking care to pull on rubber gloves, so as not to "infect" the evidence, Shanlian carefully pulled the blanket down to examine her.

Her face was bloody and bruised. Over her left eye in particular, extending back to her ear and down to her cheek, was one reddish and bluish bruise, like a giant discolored birthmark. There were also multiple lacerations. The eye had received so much trauma, it appeared to have swelled shut as a result.

Around her neck was a necklace with a small cocaine spoon attached. Now that was interesting. Maybe this was a drug-related murder. Continuing his examination, Shanlian saw that the victim was wrapped in a bedspread, which was black in color with a green and pink flower design imprinted on it.

The woman wore black Chic brand pants pulled down and around her left ankle. Her socks were black in color. She wore only one left shoe, black Guess brand. The victim's red underpants had been pulled down, wrapped around her left thigh near the vagina. They had certainly been pulled down for a reason; it was too early in the investigation to tell why.

Her stomach had two small brownish and blackish wounds, about three inches in diameter. Farther down, there was a small bruise on her right thigh, then another circular wound up near the vagina. Finally, on the inner side of the right ankle, Shanlian discovered a fifth wound, again about three inches in diameter, brownish and blackish in color.

The victim was wearing a maroon-colored, short-sleeved polo shirt with SOUTH BOULEVARD STATION emblazoned over the left breast. Neither shirt nor bra appeared to have been disturbed. If she'd been raped, the killer had not touched her breasts.

On her arms, right on top of the right biceps, was what appeared to be a burn mark. Had the woman been tortured before she died? Underneath the arm, in the arm joint, was a second burn mark, though this appeared more like a brownish or blackish wound. There was frayed skin and discoloration around her right wrist consistent with a ligature wound. That is, someone had bound her wrist before she died.

Shanlian picked up her right hand and noticed a gold-colored ring with a large sapphire on her ring finger. Underneath her fingernail was blood and something else. Forensics would take those scrapings; hopefully, they'd lead to something.

Shanlian didn't see any injuries on her left arm, though her left fingernails had blood underneath them. Her left thumbnail and part of the tip of the thumb had a large cut on it. This was consistent with defensive wounds. But the cut appeared to have teeth marks on it. Had someone bitten her to get her to stop defending herself?

As with the right wrist, the left had a ligature wound, too. Unless forensics could offer another explanation, that meant she had been bound before she died.

"Let's turn her," Shanlian said.

He and Melki reached down and turned her onto her stomach.

There was no clue under her, no weapon, no anything except blanket and earth. They pulled up her shirt to examine her back.

Shanlian saw that it was a speckled shade of red indicating lividity; that is, a settling of the blood into that region. Since lividity had already set in, and rigor mortis, the stiffness that immediately accompanies death, had receded, it was safe to assume that she had been dead for over thirty hours. Unless, of course, someone had thrown her into a freezer to slow the whole "decomp" process down, which would completely foul things up.

Shanlian surmised that the victim's attire was consistent with that of a waitress, someone who probably worked for a business called South Boulevard Station. If the killer was trying to make sure that identification was difficult, he never should have left the shirt on. Then again, he probably figured quite rightly that if the body burned, there would be no shirt left.

Searching through her pockets, Shanlian came up empty. No identification whatsoever. She also had no purse, no backpack, no nothing. Considering that she still had her ring on, they could eliminate robbery as a motive.

Today was Friday, casual day, and Shanlian had dressed in an open-necked sport shirt with jeans. When he had gotten the call, he had thrown on his sweater and overcoat and had raced to the scene. Now, he pulled his overcoat tighter around himself, but it did nothing to keep the chill out. Maybe he was getting too old for this work. Or maybe it was just the viciousness of the murder he was trying to keep out.

Shanlian stopped his musings. That was a luxury for another time. He reached inside his jacket to his belt, reminding himself that he had brought his gun.

He pulled out his cell phone; he always carried it with him now. It was de rigueur police equipment, a Nextel phone, broadcasting over digital lines so slaphappy hackers couldn't listen in on the scrambled channels like they did on scanners. Most surveillance these days was done the same way and for the same reasons.

His digital call was to the county's on-duty medical examiner, Dr. Wilys Mueller. He gave him permission to move the body. When the techies and police photographer were finished, the body would be transported to the county morgue. He also called Sergeant Ives Potrafka of his department and requested he come to the crime scene as soon as possible. Then it was a quick call to the on-duty county prosecutor, David Newblatt, who authorized the autopsy for the following morning at 11:00.

Next up was a check of missing person reports. Shanlian called the Flint Police and Central Dispatch and requested a search of all recent missing W/F reports that matched the victim's description.

That brought negative results quickly: he could find no one missing who fit the dead woman's description. Shanlian responded with a Statewide Administrative message, what used to be known as an All Points Bulletin (APB), requesting information on any recent missing person reports. Trying to match those to the victim also proved a negative result.

Sometimes, bad guys are captured on videotape before they commit the murder. There was one case in Tampa, Florida, where a serial killer named Sam Smithers walked into a convenience store with his victim, bought some stuff, and less than a half hour later killed her. The tape allowed the prosecutors to put him together with the victim before the murder took place. Shanlian requested that detectives retrieve any video surveillance from area gas stations.

A few minutes later, Sergeant Ives Potrafka of the sheriff's office arrived on the scene to assist Shanlian.

"Ives, I want you to maintain the crime scene in order to free up other detectives for further investigation."

It was a boring but important job; Potrafka had to maintain the integrity of the scene, not allow anyone to contaminate it and make sure that any evidence gathered by the Michigan Police Crime

Lab found its way to Shanlian immediately. Most importantly, Potrafka would be in charge of making sure the body got transported to the morgue after the crime scene was completely processed.

Looking down at the victim's T-shirt, Shanlian knew he didn't have to be a Ph.D. to figure out what was next. He asked a female deputy to call all the local area codes and see if she could locate a restaurant called South Boulevard Station. She came back a few minutes later with the answer. There was a restaurant by that name in Auburn Hills.

Auburn hills. That was only an hour's drive south. Shanlian hypothesized that maybe she was killed down there and dumped in his bailiwick. He wouldn't know for sure until he went down there.

Other True Crime Classics
from Fred Rosen

Body Dump   ISBN: 0-7860-1133-5

Hooker Hunter

In October 1996, women began vanishing off the streets of Poughkeepsie, New York. All were young, pretty, and petite. Most were hustlers and crack-heads. By August 1998, as the toll reached eight, a victim's mother said bitterly, "When they find one, they'll find them all." She didn't know how horrifyingly right she was.

Hulking and Homicidal

At the height of the manhunt, prostitute Christine Sala, hysterical, told police she had barely escaped being strangled by Kendall Francois, 27, a 6'4", 300-pound middle school hall monitor whose slovenly personal hygiene had earned him the nickname "Stinky." When caught, Francois said that he'd killed the women because they hadn't given him all the sex he claimed he'd paid for.

House of Horrors

Investigators in white biohazard suits entered the house where Francois lived and found eight female corpses, almost all decomposed. Some were placed in plastic bags together in the attic. Others lay in shallow graves in the crawl space under the house. It was such a tangle of rotting flesh and bones even the investigators couldn't tell how many bodies there were. Now, sentenced to life in prison without parole, the man whom others dismissed as a smelly oaf had finally been unmasked as one of the most bizarre serial sex-killers of modern times.

Includes 16 Pages of Disturbing Photos

Lobster Boy   ISBN: 0-7860-1569-1

Carny Celebrity

Descended from a notorious carny family, Grady Stiles Jr. led an unusual life. Trading on the deformity that gave his hands and feet the appearance of lobster claws, he achieved fame and fortune as "Lobster Boy," promoting himself and other carnival acts such as "Midget Man," and even his own stepson, Glenn Newman, Jr., "The Human Blockhead."

Criminal Conspiracy

But beneath Stiles's grotesque sideshow persona lurked a violent man who secretly abused his family for years, until his wife and stepson decided to do something about it—by entering into a conspiracy to kill. On November 29, 1992, as the wheelchair-bound Stiles sat watching TV in his Gibsonton, Florida, trailer home, Christopher Wyant stole in and shot him three times in the back of the head. Wyant's fee for the murder was $1,500.

Courtroom Circus

In one of the most sensational murder trials ever to make national news—a trial complete with star witnesses from the carny world, controversial evidence and courtroom handwalks by Stiles's deformed son—Mary Teresa Stiles, Glenn Newman, Jr. and Christopher Wyant were convicted of murder and sentenced to multiple prison terms.

Includes 16 Pages of Disturbing Photos

ABOUT THE AUTHOR

Fred Rosen is a former columnist for the *New York Times*. He is the author of thirteen true crime books, including the classic *Lobster Boy*.

Lobster Boy is currently in development with Joe Berlinger, director of *Blair Witch 2* and the documentaries *Brother's Keeper* and *Paradise Lost: The Child Murders at Robin Hood Hills*. *Chameleon*, a book he cowrote about a Canadian undercover agent, is being developed as a movie of the week for Canadian television.

Mr. Rosen studied film at the legendary film school of the University of Southern California, where he received his M.F.A. in cinema. His film credits include associate producer on *Pitch People*, an award-winning documentary that played many of the country's major film festivals.

He is currently an adjunct associate professor of criminal justice at Ulster County Community College.

MORE MUST-READ TRUE CRIME
FROM PINNACLE

Slow Death 0-7860-1199-8 $6.50US/$8.99CAN
By James Fielder

Fatal Journey 0-7860-1578-0 $6.50US/$8.99CAN
By Jack Gieck

Partners in Evil 0-7860-1521-7 $6.50US/$8.99CAN
By Steve Jackson

Dead and Buried 0-7860-1517-9 $6.50US/$8.99CAN
By Corey Mitchell

Perfect Poison 0-7860-1550-0 $6.50US/$8.99CAN
By M. William Phelps

Family Blood 0-7860-1551-9 $6.50US/$8.99CAN
By Lyn Riddle

Available Wherever Books Are Sold!

Visit our website at **www.kensingtonbooks.com**.

HORRIFYING TRUE CRIME
FROM PINNACLE BOOKS

Body Count
by Burl Barer   0-7860-1405-9   **$6.50**US/**$8.50**CAN

The Babyface Killer
by Jon Bellini   0-7860-1202-1   **$6.50**US/**$8.50**CAN

Love Me to Death
by Steve Jackson   0-7860-1458-X   **$6.50**US/**$8.50**CAN

The Boston Stranglers
by Susan Kelly   0-7860-1466-0   **$6.50**US/**$8.50**CAN

Body Double
by Don Lasseter   0-7860-1474-1   **$6.50**US/**$8.50**CAN

The Killers Next Door
by Joel Norris   0-7860-1502-0   **$6.50**US/**$8.50**CAN

Available Wherever Books Are Sold!

Visit our website at **www.kensingtonbooks.com**.

BOOK YOUR PLACE ON OUR WEBSITE AND MAKE THE READING CONNECTION!

We've created a customized website just for our very special readers, where you can get the inside scoop on everything that's going on with Zebra, Pinnacle and Kensington books.

When you come online, you'll have the exciting opportunity to:

- View covers of upcoming books
- Read sample chapters
- Learn about our future publishing schedule (listed by publication month *and author*)
- Find out when your favorite authors will be visiting a city near you
- Search for and order backlist books from our online catalog
- Check out author bios and background information
- Send e-mail to your favorite authors
- Meet the Kensington staff online
- Join us in weekly chats with authors, readers and other guests
- Get writing guidelines
- AND MUCH MORE!

Visit our website at http://www.kensingtonbooks.com